# GREEK VASES

# Classical World Series

Classical World Series

# GREEK VASES

## an introduction

Elizabeth Moignard

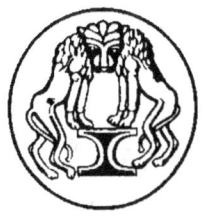

Bristol Classical Press

**Published by Bristol Classical Press 2012**

Bristol Classical Press, an imprint of Bloomsbury Publishing Plc

Bloomsbury Publishing Plc
50 Bedford Square
London WC1B 3DP
www.bloomsburyacademic.com

Copyright © Elizabeth Moignard 2006

First published by Gerald Duckworth & Co. Ltd. 2006

The author has asserted her rights under the Copyright, Designs and
Patents Act 1988 to be identified as the author of this work.

ISBN: 978 1 853 99691 7

A CIP catalogue record for this book is available from the British Library

Typeset by Ray Davies

# Contents

# Illustrations

# Acknowledgements

First, I should like to thank Michael Gunningham and Deborah Blake for commissioning this book for the Classical World Series, and the anonymous readers of my first draft, who made some sane, helpful, and improving suggestions. Writing it has provided a focus for some thoughts which I have had for some time, in a context in which I have also been teaching undergraduates, and examining for AQA. I should like also, therefore, to thank my fellow examiners for Classical Civilisation at A-level, who have been inspiring colleagues; my students, who have been receptive and thought-provoking; my colleagues both at Glasgow University and in the wider classical community, who have been happy to let me talk about an absorbing hobby as well as a professional concern, and have sometimes come to listen and react. I should also like to thank the scholars who taught me, especially Donna Kurtz, John Boardman and Martin Robertson, and my husband Alec Yearling for listening, looking, and providing both constructive criticism and support for a very short twenty years.

E.M.

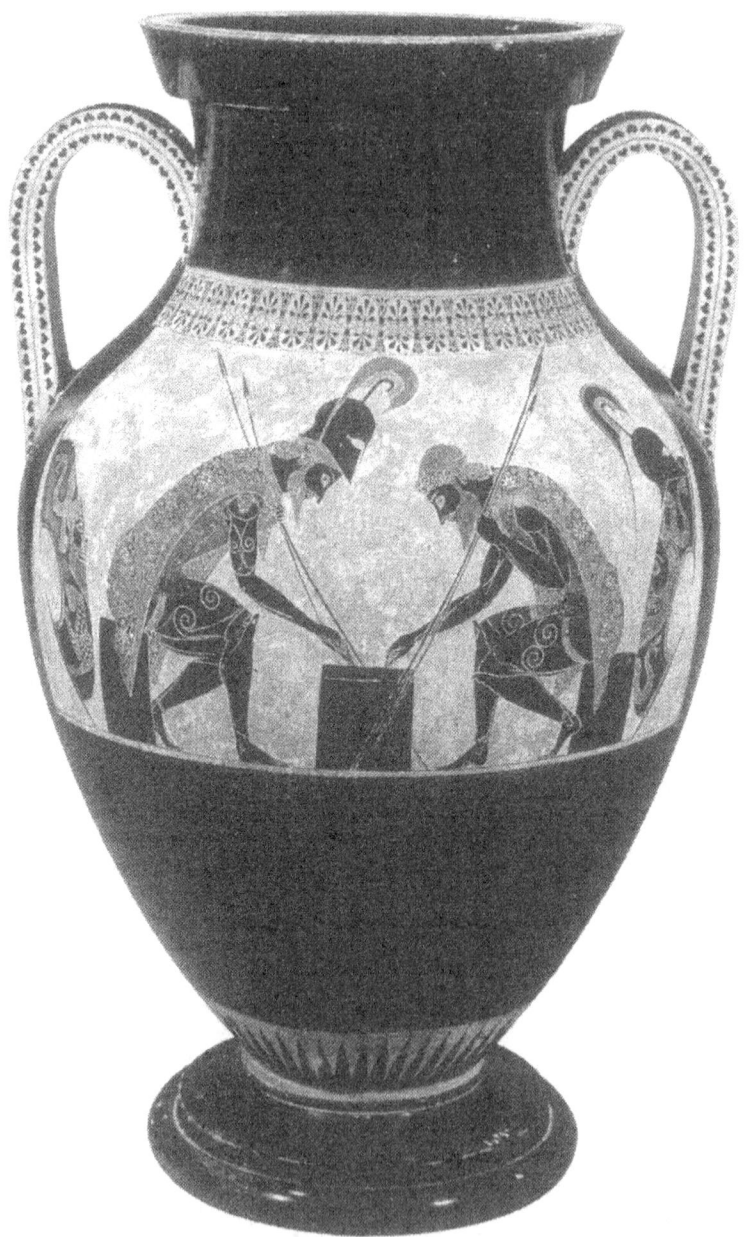

Fig. 1. Ajax and Achilles playing a board game. Athenian black-figure amphora painted by Exekias. *c.* 540-530 BC. Vatican Museums, Rome. H. 61 cm.

# Preface

Fig. 1 is a picture of a famous Greek vase which is often used as an illustration in a wide range of classical textbooks, even those not primarily concerned with Greek art. The caption tells you that it is an Athenian black-figure amphora of around 540-530 BC, painted by Exekias, and showing Ajax and Achilles playing a board game. If you were to see the vase itself, in the Vatican Museum in Rome, this is more or less what the label would say too. But it would also tell you that it was found, not in or around Athens, but at Vulci, in Etruria, north of Rome itself. The vase itself is displayed with many more like it, and this is true of other big museums all over the world. We tend to accept all of this without thinking about it very much, but if you think about it, you will see that there are questions that it raises. Why is it there at all? Why are Greek vases collected? Are they works of art? Are they valuable? And if we think about the information on the label, some of that is mystifying too: how do we know the date? Or where it came from, especially if it was found somewhere else? What does 'black-figure' mean? What is an amphora? Who was Exekias? How do we know that the figures are Ajax and Achilles? A pot is a strange place to draw figures, and the figures are perhaps a little strange-looking. Why do people bother with Greek vases at all? Why are they special in some way?

This book will to try to answer these questions, and by doing so it will also look at how vases are used as archaeological evidence, how we give them dates, and what they tell us about the societies which produced and used them. We shall look at the ways in which we generally see Greek vases, how they are published, and the techniques we use for organising and referring to them. Many publications refer to the artist who painted a particular vase, and we shall look at some of the more important painters, and their work. We shall look at the way in which picture and pattern making on Greek vases developed over a long period of time, and also at the way in which we study the subject matter of those pictures, and the way in which stories are related through them. A final chapter will discuss the history of collecting Greek vases, their publication, and their importance to the history of art and archaeology.

**Chronology and terminology**

Although chronological strategies will be discussed in Chapter 1, I have used a conventional framework in using dates elsewhere in this book, with the names we usually give to periods and styles. So the dates are:

| | |
|---|---|
| tenth century | 999-900 BC |
| ninth century | 899-800 BC |
| eighth century | 799-700 BC |
| seventh century | 699-600 BC |
| sixth century | 599-500 BC |
| fifth century | 499-400 BC |
| fourth century | 399-300 BC |

Broadly speaking *Protogeometric* pottery belongs in the tenth century, *Geometric* in the ninth to late eighth century; the styles of the late eighth and seventh centuries are known as *Orientalising*. *Black-figure* appears in Corinth in the early to middle seventh century, and lasts in the cities which use it till the early fifth century, except for specialised uses which may go on later. *Red-figure* appears in Athens in the late sixth century, and lasts until it fades out in the Southern Italian cities in the late fourth century BC.

*Archaic* is the term used for the period of Greek history from about the middle of the seventh century BC until the Persian invasions of 490 and 480 BC, and you may find it used to describe art from that period. Similarly *Classical* is used to mean the period between 480 and the death of Alexander the Great in 323 BC, and the art produced in that period.

*Attica* is the territory of the Athenians, including the city of Athens; *Attic* is the adjective which describes the people, their city and country-side, and their material culture, including pottery.

# Chapter 1

## Greek Vases and Time

How do we study and use Greek vases today? Although we may enjoy their appearance or the content and style of their pictures, we also treat them as speaking objects, which can tell us a story about their makers and owners, and their lives and priorities. They appear as part of the visual and material evidence for the study of the society which produced them, and they may support, amplify, or complicate, the textual evidence which we also have for the period. The work which they are required to do includes:

- Archaeological evidence as part of the find-catalogue from a site, and thus evidence for, among other things trade, production, population movement.
- Visual support, or even the starting point, for the study of domestic history, especially, at any rate recently, female history.
- Visual support for the study of the use and wear of everyday material objects, dress or tools for which we have little other evidence.
- Primary evidence for the reception, development and use of mythological structures and concepts, whether in ritual or secular activity.
- The study, anthropological or descriptive reportage, of burial and other ritual customs, especially those which involve physical remains.
- The development of narrative, both visual and verbal.
- The development of certain kinds of craft skills.
- The beginning of some visual and conceptual skills which can be seen to extend over a much longer period and into other media, such as approaches to perspective drawing
- Communication of ideas and concepts to an informed and receptive contemporary public, whether contemporary with the production of the pots, or to us.

And that is only in the study of the ancient world; there is also the later history of the study of these objects, where they supply, or have supplied, interior decoration, supported an art market, and filled museums, and thereby now provide professional material on several fronts for a wide variety of practitioners. The list above indicates many different sorts of interest with many different backgrounds – several different sorts of researching and teaching academic and not just those who study the ancient Greek world, museum staff, craft practitioners, archaeologists, film makers, designers.

## Why we study Greek vases

We may find it helpful if we look at two important ways in which we study and use Greek vases in order to understand the context in which they were produced. First of all, they are like any other ancient pottery: they are a domestic commodity which, when dug up on an archaeological site, can be interpreted to tell us about the way in which people lived, about their trade, their eating and drinking habits, and possibly something about the dates at which they were doing all this. But many Greek vases, like our Ajax and Achilles amphora, have pictures on them, which makes them a specialised type of archaeological ceramic, and it also means that they have a history of being viewed as works of art too. The very fact that we often call these pots vases, a more dignified signifier, is part of a tradition, established since the sixteenth century AD, of collecting them as examples of the visual art of the civilisation which produced them, and, more recently, approaching them as the work of distinguishable individuals, despite the absence of contemporary accounts of either pots or the workshops which produced them.

A very large part of their popularity as a collectable is that there are a great many of them, and this is one reason for their usefulness as an archaeological object too. Pottery is the largest single category of human artefact found on any Mediterranean, and particularly eastern Mediterranean, site. The Greeks buried large numbers of pots with their dead; the funeral party often left its drinking utensils behind in the grave or tomb, together with vases containing oil and sometimes food (so we have a wide variety of types of vase) together with other sorts of item. Graves are where most of our surviving vases come from. Urban and domestic sites tend to produce broken items discarded as rubbish, and the kind of pieces which come from such an archaeological context are often not the best examples of their type, or may be plain pieces produced for kitchen use. Much of the best work of the Greek potter and painter was specifically produced for funerary use, or for other grand occasions, and in some cases was buried at second-hand.

## How archaeologists approach vases

Greek pots, for the archaeologist, form an important part of the evidence for the chronology of the sites they excavate. Pots cannot provide all the evidence needed by themselves, but can be linked with other types of evidence, including the work of historical writers such as Herodotus and Thucydides, associations with other kinds of material artefact, datable buildings, and parallels with other visual material which is more easily datable. Pottery is the largest single class of artefact found on any Mediterranean site; it is also the least destructible. It may be broken, but it does not break down organically, and with care, it can be reconstructed; one of the first tasks on a traditional excavation is to try to reassemble broken ceramic vessels – a sort of three-dimensional jig-saw.

Fig. 18 (p. 41) shows a burial vase from the big Iron Age cemetery in Athens; it was reassembled from numerous sherds, as were most of the other vessels from tombs in this burial ground. Even if it proves impossible to get this far, if the fragments can be identified in terms of date, source and the shape of which they were part, we can tell much about the site and its inhabitants' history which is not recorded in any written source. A great deal is known about Greek pottery, although there is still much to learn, and its presence, and the sheer amount of it, on Mediterranean sites, has fuelled very detailed studies of its styles, changing appearance over time, distribution in terms of trade, either of the pots themselves or of their contents, and of the potters and painters who made them in the first place.

One aim of the excavating archaeologist has often been to relate the finds from the excavation site to real dates and events; the archaeological record of ancient Greece has often been treated as support for historical events recorded in the surviving textual material. Sometimes this can only be broad support for overall perceptions of cultural development and movement such as trade connections, a need for the foundation of colonies overseas, contacts with other peoples outside the Mediterranean area, major wars. Very occasionally, a particular site can yield material which can be linked very closely with a specific and datable historical event. Among these are graves which can be linked with battles or campaigns, themselves capable of precise dating, and foundation or destruction evidence from settlements and sanctuaries.

Probably the best known mass war-grave is the mound at Marathon which was built to hold the remains of the men who died on the battlefield fighting the invading Persians in 490 BC. The historians Herodotus (6.117) and Thucydides (2.34.5) are the most detailed source of information about the dead: they tell us that 192 Athenians were killed there, and that because of the distinction of their service, they were buried on the battlefield. The mound has been partially excavated, and the interpretation of the finds has not been straightforward; in general, though, there is a consensus that the finds represent offerings made to those who died shortly after the battle. A large proportion of the finds consist of Attic black-figure pottery; there were also a fragment of a Attic red-figure cup, and other ceramic material of earlier date or non-Attic origin. The Attic black-figure pottery from this site provides a check against which both similar items and the stylistic sequence of Attic black-figure as a whole can be measured.

Another, later example comes from the Kerameikos cemetery in Athens, which contains both public and private graves. In the private sector is the relief marker commemorating Dexileos, who was killed fighting as a cavalry officer at Corinth in 394 BC. He was buried with his fellow cavalrymen in a state grave, but at the time of his death his family came into possession of the corner site where the relief stands; five red-figure oinochoai (see Chapter 3 for vase shapes), which may have been deposited at the time it was set up, are often used as indicators of the stylistic development of Attic red-figure at the time. The fact that one of them shows the Tyrant-slayers, in a pose which relates closely to the statue group in the Athenian Agora, allows for comparison with other representations which contribute to chronological considerations.

A third important chronological and stylistic sequence, which connects a written source with a pottery style, is that built around the foundation of the Greek colonies of Southern Italy and Sicily. Thucydides (6.3-5) is our major historical source for the dating of these foundations, for which he provides a relative chronology by linking them to one another. An essential link in the chain is the destruction of Megara Hyblaea by Gelon of Syracuse, 245 years after its foundation. Gelon's career can be dated from other sources with some precision, and so can the destruction of Megara, to within about a year, which then establishes its foundation date. On the basis of Thucydides and other sources, the foundation dates of most of the Western Greek colonies can be established with some precision. With this goes the assumption that the earliest pots found on the site in any numbers can be assumed to be among the earliest years of the city's existence. In this case, Corinthian pottery predominates: the seventh- and sixth-century styles known as Protocorinthian and Corinthian, which form a stylistic sequence, link with the foundation dates of the colonies to provide a widely accepted dating sequence. This is in itself important, because the wide distribution of the pottery can also provide evidence for the dates of other kinds of material. A fragment in the foundations or fill of a building can indicate the date of its construction.

These examples are, of course, only three from a number of datable contexts of this sort, and we need to be aware of the difficulties of precision; burying pottery as grave-goods with the dead involves a choice of items, some of which may have been used in life for some time before their deposit. A belief system which involved, as these burials show, a sense that afterlife in the Underworld was in some ways a version of the life the dead lived above ground, meant that the dead were buried with a range of possessions, some of them heirlooms. Larger and more elaborate vessels, some of them not native to the site, might be a generation or more earlier than the rest of the grave group. This will also be true of finds from shrines or domestic sites, which usually reflect a long period of use or votive practice before the events which led to their destruction or abandonment. Confidence in the dates provided by ancient historians for the earlier periods of Greek civilisation is not complete; some of the colonial sites have produced Corinthian pottery which should belong to an earlier point in the sequence than the foundation date indicated by Thucydides. Some archaeologists and historians have therefore begun to question the assumption that the earliest pottery indicates the earliest settlers on any site. And foreign pottery might be imports rather than colonists' baggage. Religious and political centres probably provide the soundest evidence: if they are excavated to their bottom levels, there can be some confidence that the earliest material is there. The context and the interpretation of the finds is crucially important.

## How we study pots without dates

A related way to look at Greek pots is to take a developmental approach – that is to see how they change over the passage of time, and how their shapes and systems of decoration change. An archaeologist will try to establish the pattern of such changes for the particular site he studies, both for local pottery and imports, and this will have important consequences for the eventual view he will take of the dating of the site, who was there, and what foreign contacts were made, and when. What the pottery specialist on an excavation tries to establish is the sequence, and this depends on an accepted dating system, established by the methods exemplified earlier, for certain kinds of easily-identified pots, on which most people are prepared to agree. This in itself pre-supposes that that most potters and decorators were conservative in style and stuck to the sequence of change: we can allow for failures and hurried or mass-produced items, but genuinely individualist pieces and experiments may upset the sequence. Fig. 2 shows three variants on the one-piece Athenian amphora

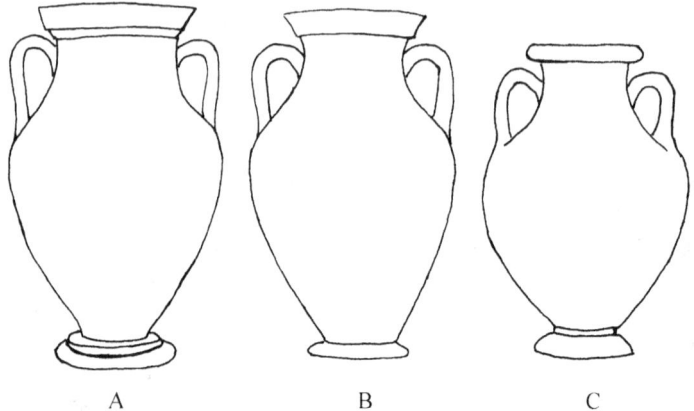

A                    B                    C

Fig. 2. Late archaic Attic amphora shapes. Type A amphora, *c*. 540 BC. Type B amphora, *c*. 500 BC. Type C amphora, *c*. 470 BC.

from the mid-eighth to the mid-fifth century BC. Type A has flanged handles, Types B and C cylindrical ones. We can put relative dates to the introduction of the three types; the type A amphora, it is sometimes argued, was Exekias' contribution to its evolution – a designer name. Each of the three shapes has its own pattern of gradual and subtle change over time, which will help a dating sequence. The archaeologist tries to establish this kind of sequence without the aid of records, but by careful drawing and comparison. This is where not only shape studies, but the study of developing decorative styles, and even painters, comes in. Better still, if we can attach a real date to one pot, by association of similar objects with a datable site or event, then we can date the rest of the sequence, at least roughly, too. This is how the date 540-530 BC was arrived at for our Exekias amphora, and also why it is a ten-year period, and not a particular year. What is also important to our time framework is that there is a strong connection between the developing styles of pottery and the identifiable craftsmen who made them; Exekias signed his work, as did a number of other makers. Even when they remain anonymous, the developing design tradition to which they and their clients contributed is an important contributor to our sense of the chronology of our pottery series.

## Styles and chronology

Many of the uses we make of the study of Greek pottery have more to do with its evolving style, in relation to the technique and content of its pictures, if any. The study of these aspects of the material, with some reference to datable pieces, is how we arrive at a large-scale stylistic time-sequence for decorated Greek pots which begins roughly in the tenth century BC, as Greece recovered from the destruction of its Bronze age civilisation, and goes on till the fading-out of figured vases in the fourth century BC. The earliest decorated pottery already has the seeds of the sort of skills and schemes which become so characteristic later.

Fig. 3 shows an amphora from an Athenian burial of the tenth century BC in the Protogeometric style; the shape is one which appears with decoration on the shoulder and belly of the vase. Earlier examples have concentric circles in the major pattern-locations, but a few have a wave pattern as this one does. This particular vessel begins a new decorative tradition by showing a small stylised horse at one end of the wave. Before long, many burial vessels will have figure decoration: first repeated stylised animals, and then human figures engaged in a recognisable activity.

Much is now beginning to be read into the scenes on Geometric vases, but I think it remains true to say that the first figure scenes are specifically for funeral use, and show funeral scenes. A little later there are battles, which may well be there to honour the dead because they fell in battle, or because their families wished they had, and died a heroic death, and sometimes there are chariot processions. Almost all these early pictures are Athenian (and it is important to remember that the Athenians were the

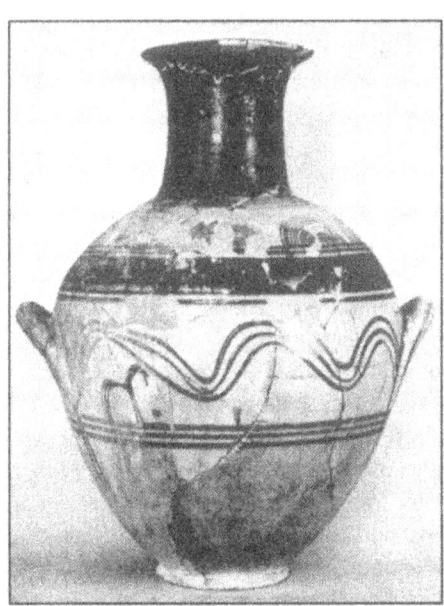

Fig. 3. Protogeometric amphora from the Kerameikos cemetery, tenth century BC. Kerameikos Museum, Athens. H. 47.2 cm.

great developers of storytelling in pictures), and they often appear on the sides of very large vases which acted as grave-markers, intended to be highly visible to any passer-by.

The amphora known by its museum number as Athens 804 (Figs 18, 19) has a scene which is not only a very stylised representation of a funeral, but is also one of the very earliest pictures, in a frame. It dates from about 750 BC, and it belongs towards the end of the Geometric period; it is also by a painter whose work can be recognised elsewhere. Notice the way in which the figures are stylised, and made to be part of the pattern. This is not primitive drawing, but a very sophisticated decorative system. But it is already a restrictive one for the artist, especially if he is interested in telling stories, and we should not be surprised to find that something much less stylised takes its place. What we have seen here, though, is pottery become an established place to draw people, and this is what develops.

About the time this vase was made, the population of Greece seems to have been increasing; in a mountainous country which lived by agriculture, this meant that the surplus people had to travel abroad to find other land to farm; some Greeks had already migrated to the west coast of what is now Turkey and were established in already well-developed cities by the end of the eighth century BC. The Greeks began to travel more, make contact with the older civilisations of the Near East and Egypt, and re-acquire lost skills or develop new ones. At the same time they were exploring to the west, especially Italy, to find raw metal ores. This is how they met the Etruscans. Meanwhile Greece itself was beginning to crystallise politically into separate city-states, and these began to develop their own distinctive styles of pottery; these then continued to evolve separately, and there was no single Greek style. Towards the end of the sixth century, Athens dominated the market and emerged as the only serious producer of figured vases. This is how being able to recognise the different styles can tell us about who was on a site, and also when.

Corinth was the most influential trading city: her geographical position, with two harbours, one on each side of the Isthmus, allowed her to develop as a trading power. Traders could avoid the dangerous voyage round the south of the Peloponnese (it is not accidental that this is where Odysseus gets blown out of the real world altogether: *Odyssey* 9.80-1), and the city stood at the junction of two major overland routes. Very quickly Corinth became the recipient of new ideas, especially decorative ones, from the east, and passed them on to others. She also became the first industrialised city, which channelled its pottery industry towards the mass-production of containers for luxury goods such as scent (Fig. 4), and the first of what we call the Orientalising styles of Greek pottery was born.

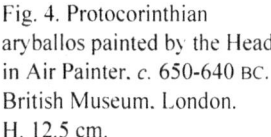

Fig. 4. Protocorinthian
aryballos painted by the Head
in Air Painter. *c.* 650-640 BC.
British Museum. London.
H. 12.5 cm.

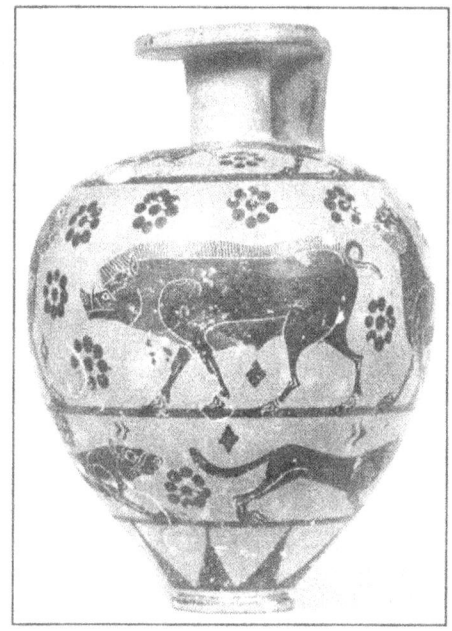

At first, the decorative style is clearly experimental, and although the creamy colour of the clay and the matte brown paint allow us to identify them as Corinthian, the shape of the bottle itself is a better indicator of origin, and a better guide to later development of the shape. Corinthian Geometric vessels were not normally decorated with figures, apart from the occasional row of birds, and many Orientalising ones, similarly, use birds and other animals, or patterns derived from plant forms. Some of these are themselves clearly of Near Eastern origin, and reflect the trading contacts inherent in Corinth's success, and also the Near Eastern objects and their decoration, which came to Greece as a result. This may also be one of the factors which underlie the gradual introduction into pottery decoration of figure scenes with a mythological content. A king or hero fighting a lion is not an uncommon feature of royal iconography in Egypt and the Near East, and it is possible that the story of Herakles and the Lion began as a small-scale illustration of such an episode on an imported decorative object, which gave rise to a local story to explain it.

Essentially, we see the pottery market in Corinth evolving in two parallel ways during the seventh and sixth centuries. If our understanding of the evidence is correct, the major impetus was towards mass production of containers, particularly for scented oils; the demands of such production led to the natural development of a characteristic form of decoration

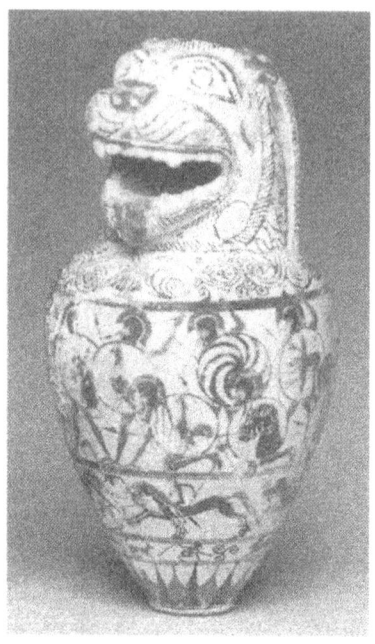

Fig. 5. The Macmillan aryballos,
Protocorinthian, painted by the Chigi
Painter, c. 640 BC. British Museum,
London. H. 6.8 cm.

which used animal and plant forms, which could be stylised in a way
which made them quick to paint. The result is often not unlike a patterned
cloth woven in horizontal stripes – indeed there is a certain amount of
evidence to suggest the existence of contemporary textiles of this kind.

There are some much rarer examples of figured pottery alongside our
animal vases from Corinth. They were presumably far more complex to
achieve, and so slower, and not susceptible to mass production, unless
extremely standardised and generic. The Macmillan aryballos (Fig. 5),
dating from around 640 BC, is one such extremely finely produced and
decorated vessel. It is a pointed aryballos – a shape-development away
from the round one which helps to determine its place in the shape-series.
Despite the fact that it stands only around 7 cm high, it carries three figured
friezes: a pitched infantry battle, a horse race, and a hare hunt, all painted
in great detail with a sure command of technique and compositional skill.

The painter can be identified as the creator of a number of other equally
accomplished and delicate pieces of work, mainly on small vessels,
though there is a jug, known as the Chigi vase, which has two files of
infantry advancing on each other with a piper to keep them in formation.
None of this painter's work could be described as mass-produced, but
there are other figured vessels from seventh- and sixth-century Corinth
which use simpler, and usually cruder, figure-scenes, including shield-

bearing warriors marching into battle. These can be seen as an equivalent of the animal vases, serving a mass market in the same way. By the middle of the sixth century BC both animal and figure styles are showing signs of wear and tear; the animals, in particular, become longer and longer in the body, and the ornaments around them increasingly careless. Longer animals mean fewer need be painted to reach around the pot, and little effort is expended on the detail of animals, human figures, or plant decoration.

By the last thirty years of the seventh century BC, the technique which we call black-figure was making painting both kinds of decoration, but especially the animal patterns, in a durable form, much easier to achieve. The clays used by most Greek potters and painters were rich in iron, which can be fired to produce a spectrum of colours from creamy-buff to deep orange-red. A concentrated form of the same clay, used as a paint or glaze and put through a more complex and extended firing process, can be induced to turn brown or black. As it becomes integral to the vessel surface as part of the firing process, it is extremely durable. The painter can score through it to the contrasting surface beneath to produce an incised line which can play the same role in the depiction of a figure as a drawn line. The result is a form of drawing which uses black figures on a paler, often red, background, with added incised details and, often, added red or white slip for emphasis or, eventually, gender differentiation.

The Athenians adopted black-figure not long after it appeared in Corinth, and developed a much more sophisticated use for it. During the seventh and sixth centuries they extended what was a local taste for narrative art, the descendant of their Geometric figure scenes, into a fully developed style in which both sophisticated genre scenes and visual myth played an outstanding part. Corinthian painters developed narrative figure painting, often on their larger and more formal vessels, in the same way, but not to the same extent, and rarely to the same level of expertise.

Many other local styles of pottery, including Spartan, Boeotian and those of the East Greek cities, show an Orientalising phase with mainly animal-based decoration, and then develop a narrative figure style during the sixth century. One dominant East Greek Orientalising style is known to us as Wild Goat, because of its pre-occupation with long-horned goats as the animal of choice in its friezes. A plate in the British Museum (Fig. 6, overleaf) shows a battle over the body of Euphorbus, an episode from the Trojan War. Its style is closely related to Wild Goat, and uses the same filling-ornament. The result is effectively an all-over pattern which tends to obscure the figure scene, despite labels which tell us who the figures are; they have become part of the overall effect, and the concentration on the narrative which we see evolving in Athens is not present here.

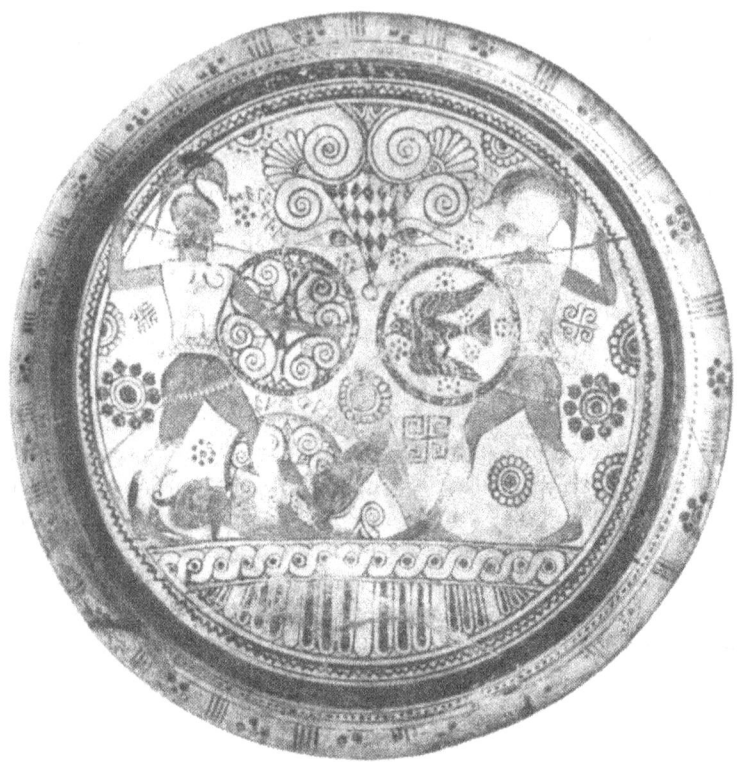

Fig. 6. Hector and Menelaos fight over the body of Euphorbus. ?Rhodian plate, late seventh century BC. British Museum, London. W. 38.5 cm.

Athens seems to have come to colonisation and trade late, and her pottery developed differently: her Orientalising vases appear highly experimental, and more interested in figures and stories than in patterns, or at least with a greater emphasis on the stories than the surrounding plant life. Painters' styles are extremely individual during the seventh century, before the adoption of black-figure. The elegant stylisations of Athenian Geometric evolved into a figure style which allowed curves, and selective use of outline rather than pure silhouette, often for faces. By the middle of the seventh century the Geometric style had virtually disappeared, and although the visual arrangement of the decoration on a large pot still tended to involve friezes and panels, the principal ones were filled with large figures. It is also evident that one lasting effect of the Geometric design consensus, in Athens as elsewhere, was a continuing sense of a right way to organise pictures and subsidiary patternwork on a pot.

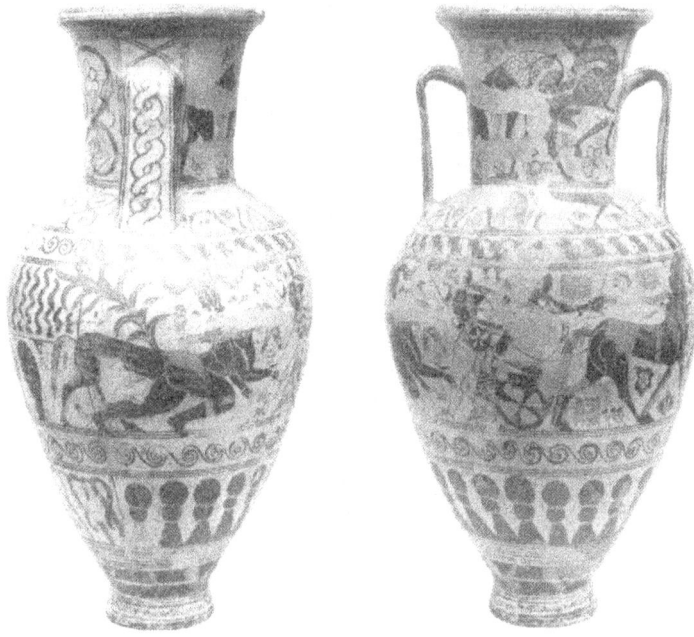

Fig. 7. Herakles and Nessos. Attic amphora painted by the New York Nessos Painter. *c.* 660 BC. Metropolitan Museum of Art. New York. H. 1.08 m.

The amphora shown in Fig. 7, known as the New York Nessos Vase, dating from around 660, was used as a grave marker, like its Geometric predecessors. It shows an interesting mixture of animal and narrative picture-making, in panels, on what was evidently intended as the side the viewer saw first. Its back is treated as a different, though related, set of spaces, and all of them have interestingly fluid and individual patterns, which are different from the ones used to frame the scenes on the front. The neck, the shoulder and the widest part of the belly are as we would expect, the place to foreground the pictures. The neck-panel shows a moon-faced carnivore, probably intended as a lion, attacking a deer. Both are drawn in a mixture of outline and silhouette with incisions, as is the elegant grazing horse on the shoulder.

The body carries not just a generic figure scene, but a representation of a specific story: the fight between Herakles and the centaur Nessos over Herakles' bride Deianeira. Again, the figures are drawn in a mixture of outline and incised silhouette, which is used effectively to differentiate Herakles both from his chariot horses, Deianeira, and the collapsing, rubbery Nessos. Herakles has a big expressive eye, as he will often have

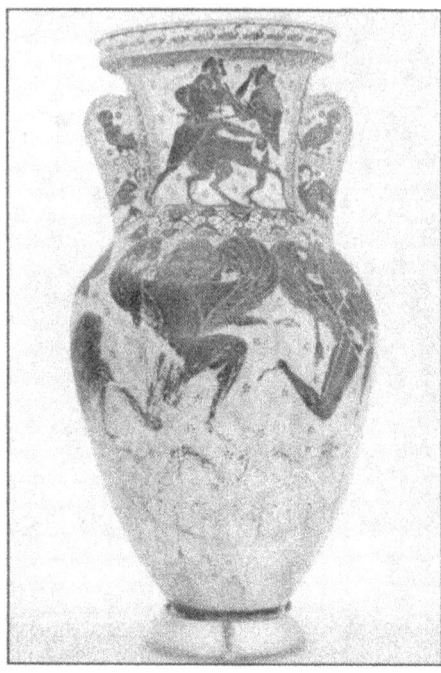

Fig. 8. Herakles and Nessos; Gorgons. Attic black-figure amphora painted by the Nessos Painter, late seventh century BC. National Archaeological Museum, Athens. H. 1.22 m.

later in Athenian painting, and much is made of Nessos' dual anatomy. The technique has been harnessed to the story in a way which becomes a major feature of later Attic painting.

By the time another version of the Nessos encounter appears on the neck panel of another grave-marker amphora (Fig. 8) of around 600 BC, black-figure is established, and Herakles and Nessos are painted in the same style. This time they have inscriptions to label them, and Herakles had a red chiton, now rubbed away. They appear alone, without Deianeira or transport, in order to fit into the square panel, overlapping each other, and the frame of the picture, which now has some of the patterns which will become standard over the next century or so. The sense of the fit between picture and the space in which it appears will be subject to experiment and evolution too. The frieze below, which shows Gorgons chasing Perseus, who has decapitated their collapsing sister Medusa, is an example of the choice of a chase or procession picture to encircle the body of a large vessel.

Other painters do this during the sixth century BC, sometimes, as on the François Vase (Fig. 9), using one frieze among many in this way, and dividing several others on the pot between front and back. The François Vase is one of the last large vessels to exhibit a taste for many friezes and

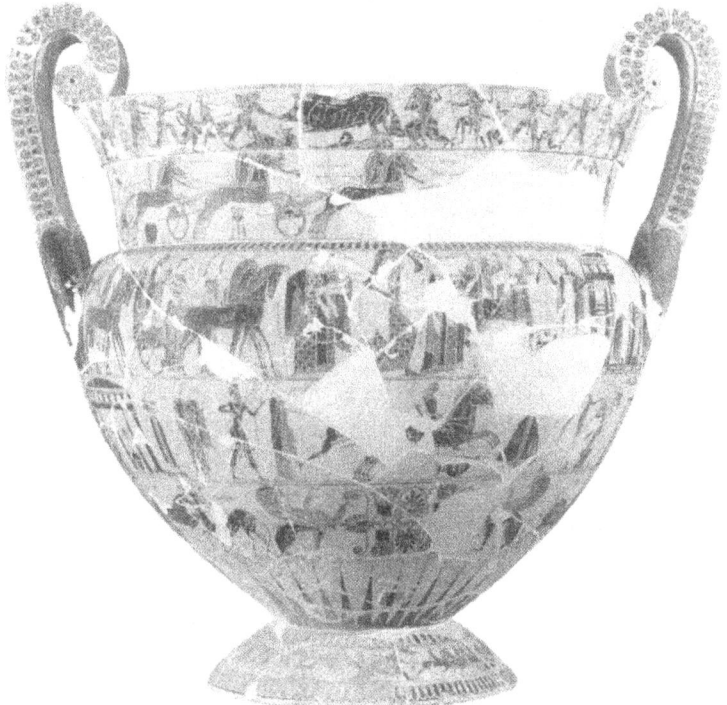

Fig. 9. The François Vase. Athenian black-figure volute krater by Kleitias and Ergotimos. c. 570 BC. Museo Archeologico. Florence. H. 66 cm.

numerous small figures, which is related to Corinthian influence, and appears alongside the large figure format in Athens until the middle of the sixth century BC.

Our Achilles and Ajax amphora (Figs 1, 34) was painted in the middle third of the sixth century, in what is usually viewed as the fully mature Athenian black-figure style. In many ways it is typical of its period and can be related closely to contemporary work by other makers. It uses each side of the vessel to show a figure scene in a panel; the figures are carefully placed, and related to the shape of the panel and to each other in a balanced composition.

The scenes, of Ajax and Achilles and on the back a departure scene with heroic personnel, may be thematically connected, but are distinct and intended to be viewed separately as a striking narrative scene. The attention to details of texture and clothing patterns, the sharp outer contours of the figures, and the clarity with which they are displayed, are all both features of this painter's style and of the highest quality work in this technique.

Even though other centres developed their own figure styles, they were rarely as sophisticated and technically accomplished as this, and in the end, it has tended to be Athenian figured vases which are desirable and collected as art. It has often been hard to remember that they are archaeological and social documents too.

All styles have their limitations, and at the end of the sixth century, black-figure had run out of steam, and red-figure, its reverse, began to replace it in Athens. Although there is a limited amount of red-figure made elsewhere during the fifth century BC, it never achieved the successes of the Athenian industry in volume or expertise. The earliest red-figure artists trained, naturally, in black-figure, and painted in both styles; the amphora illustrated in Fig. 21 (p. 49), which shows Herakles and Athena on Olympus, has a picture in each technique. At this early stage they are very similarly organised, and detailed, and it is easy to see the difference as just a reversal of the colour values from black-figure to red. It was not long, though, before painters began to develop the possibilities of what is, after all, line drawing. It was they who invented the graphic shorthand we use today for suggesting solid objects on a flat surface.

Euthymides, who signed the amphora illustrated in Fig. 22 (p. 52), is seen as one of a group of painters who were interested in developing ways of suggesting three-dimensionality via foreshortening and a careful control of the figure outlines. Red-figure afforded the opportunity to show anatomical detail and to overlap figures without loss of clarity, neither of them easy in a silhouette style. The three-quarter back view of the central figure is one of the earliest successful examples of this particular technique.

The black background of a red-figure picture militates against suggestions of depth in the picture space; by the middle of the fifth century BC some painters were trying to suggest recession and perspective, not always successfully. The Niobid Painter may have been trying to achieve the same effects as those of recorded contemporary wall-paintings on a large-format vase (Fig. 10). He manages to suggest depth by using different levels on which to place his figures, rather than putting them all on the same ground lines, but the figures which are supposedly further away should be smaller than those nearer to the viewer, by the rules of perspective drawing, and here they are on the same scale.

Little painting in other media survives from the Greek world of the classical period, though we have some ancient descriptions of some specific works of art, particularly the work of Polygnotus of Thasos, who

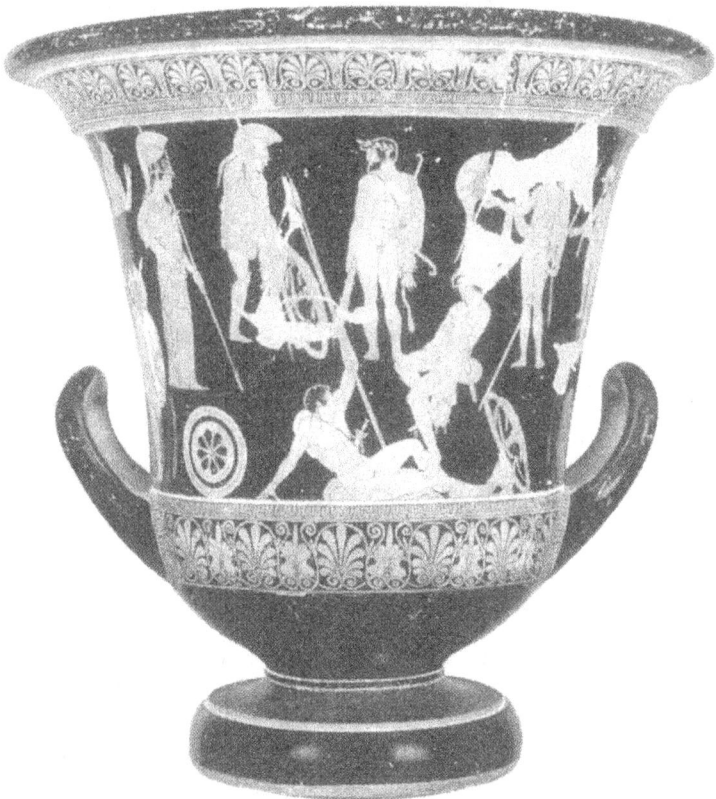

Fig. 10. Attic red-figure calyx krater painted by the Niobid Painter. c. 470-460 BC. Louvre. Paris. H. 54 cm.

was famous for his paintings of the Sack of Troy and of Odysseus in the Underworld. The surviving accounts of these suggest that they were much less dependent on violent action than on the exploration of inner motive and psychology, so that his paintings tended to feature quiet figures reflecting the implications of the myths they inhabited. Both sides of the Niobid Painter's krater show a variety of figures, many of them relatively static in rather markedly different and virtuoso poses, separated from each other in a way which invites us to consider them as individuals.

The figures in general change in style during the course of the fifth century BC, and so does their clothing. There is often a parallelism with changes in sculptural style over the same period; early fifth-century vase painting tends to an interest in surface pattern, and the figure types are close to their three-dimensional equivalents. As sculptural body propor-

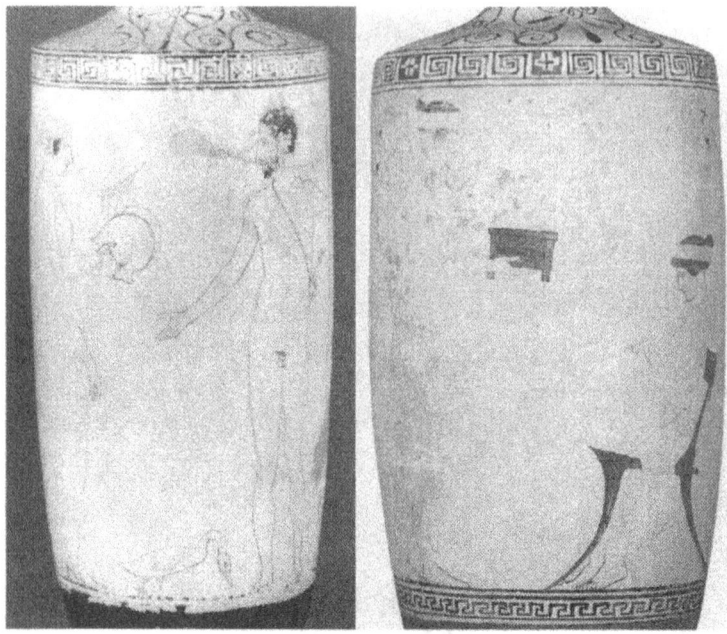

Fig. 11. Attic white-ground lekythoi painted by the Achilles Painter, *c.* 440 BC. *Left:* Woman and man, British Museum, London. *Right:* Seated woman with maid, Staatliche Antikensammlungen und Glyptothek, Munich.

tions, facial types and hairstyles change, together with fashions in clothing, so do the figures who appear on Athenian pottery. After about 460 BC, we can find a number of figures resembling the sculptures of the temple of Zeus at Olympia in physical type and clothing styles, as do the Herakles and the Athena in the Niobid Painter's scene; after 450, the evolving styles of the Parthenon sculptures and their descendants find relatives on Athenian vases. Dress is gradually depicted in a more realistic way, and then with more complex and fussy folds, and then manipulated to show the figure underneath, as if the clothing were wet. This in itself is matched by contemporary sculptural practice. The drawing is often confidently sketchy and suggestive, rather than crisp and hard-lined as it had been at the beginning of the century. Figures are shown in a more naturalistic fashion, and there is a greater interest in scenes of domestic or at least real life rather than in heroic myth. Where myths appear, there is a great interest in those which have suggestions of an afterlife, or of an escapist agenda. Women play a greater part in these scenes than they did earlier in the century.

White-ground, a technique which uses a white slip as the background to the figures, appeared for the first time as a variant on black-figure burial lekythoi, at the end of the sixth century BC (Fig. 11). The white slip rubs easily and is therefore not stable enough for pots designed to be used on a daily basis. Our best surviving examples of the technique were buried with the dead, and a number have survived in excellent condition. Not all are lekythoi, but some of the most interesting examples of fifth-century painting have survived on these oil bottles, often painted by painters who at least partly specialised in the technique. The Achilles Painter was one of the major practitioners of white-ground, and developed a series of quiet scenes in which women are seen in domestic settings, young men stand beside their tombs, warriors depart. There is a limited range of colour, browns, yellows, reds, used both for the drawn lines and for the flat colour washes. Towards the end of the century blue and green and eventually pink will appear too. The style of drawing is clearly related to the conventional red-figure of its time, but most painters working in white-ground succeed in producing a delicacy and subtlety which is not so natural to red-figure.

In the second half of the fifth century there is a noticeable shift away from the amphora as the major recipient of experimental picture making, towards the hydria and krater, which present different compositional formats for their pictures. Painters often specialise in large or small shapes, or open and closed ones, and their style and presentation is often elaborate and dramatic. A hydria by the Meidias Painter, made in the last quarter of the fifth century, is an excellent example of the taste and style of its period (Fig. 12, overleaf). It carries two different scenes, both of them illustrating myths involving potentially violent male-female inter-action in a style which does not succeed in suggesting the intensity of the story, and in fact probably was not intended to. The lower frieze shows a seated Herakles beside a very small apple tree, guarded by a very small serpent, in the Garden of the Hesperides. Between Herakles and the tree, lifting her veil in a flirtatious gesture, is one of the Hesperides. The upper frieze shows the Dioskouroi carrying off the daughters of Leukippos from a sanctuary of Aphrodite. The figures are delicately drawn, as in the lower frieze, and there is little sign of resistance to the Dioskouroi, or of force or distress. The general effect of the vase is elaborate, technically elegant, decorative and even frivolous. The seriousness of the work of our earlier painters does not appear here, and in that this painter's work is very like that of his contemporaries.

In the last third of the fifth century Athens was embroiled in a bitter war with Sparta, and although red-figure did not disappear for another hundred years or so, it could be argued that the heart had gone out of it.

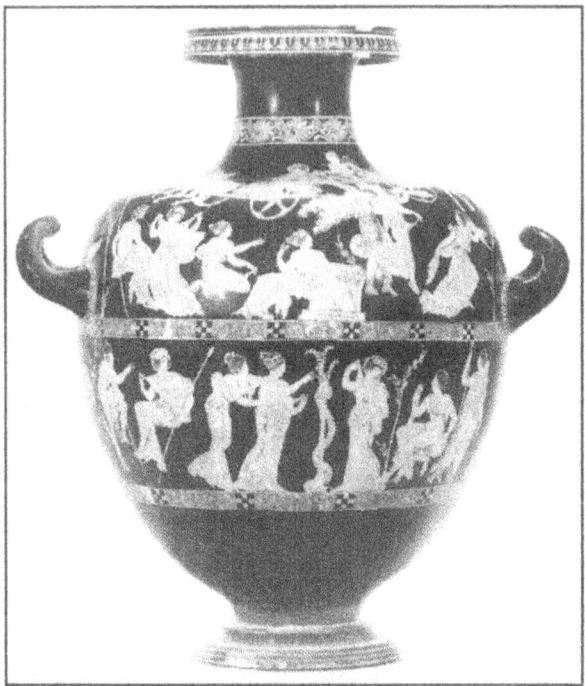

Fig. 12. Abduction of the Leukippids: Herakles in the Garden of the Hesperides. Attic red-figure hydria painted by the Meidias Painter. *c.* 420 BC. British Museum. London. H. 32.1 cm.

Some painters appear to have emigrated to Southern Italy to paint in what became a distinctive tradition of its own, again with its own patterns and problems, its own choices of subject matter and local styles, and a recognisably Greek sense of the relationship between decoration and vessel. This lasted till the end of the fourth century BC, serving a different set of social norms, with perhaps a different set of priorities.

The volute krater (Fig. 13) from Apulia in Southern Italy is a typical example of the way in which painters and potters evolved and adapted Greek vase forms and painting styles. It already has even more elaborate handles than its Greek forebears, and its picture is painted in an equally elaborate, frothy style which can be related to late Athenian paintings such as the Meidias Painter's Hesperides picture, but makes more use of added colours. This one shows Orestes at Delphi, defended from the Furies by Apollo; the figures are shown with theatrical gestures and postures. Most commentators feel that it illustrates Aeschylus' presentation of this moment in the *Eumenides*; it may even be related to a performance of it, rather than just representing its narrative. Both style and subject matter are already typical of Southern Italian vases, ornate, eye-catching, and much less restrained even than their latest Athenian predecessors.

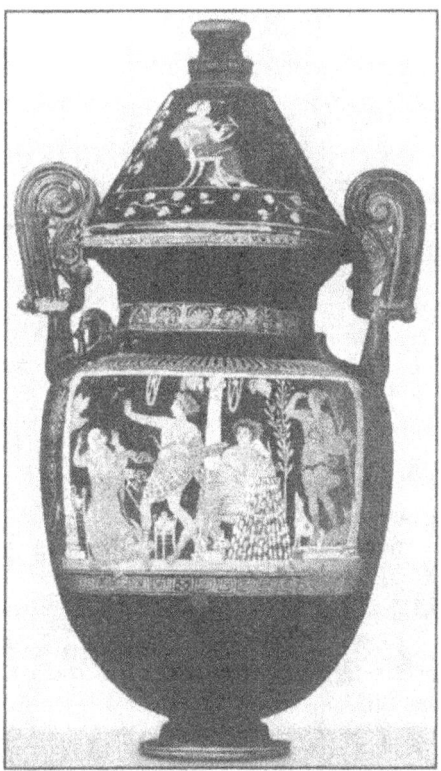

Fig. 13. Orestes at Delphi. Apulian red-figure volute krater. *c.* 370 BC. Museo Nazionale Archeologico. Naples. H. 90 cm.

# Chapter 2

# Painters and Potters

The amphora showing the board game (Fig. 1) is identified as the work of a painter and potter called Exekias; a look at the standard reference books on Greek pottery will show us that there are other vessels attributed to him, some just as a painter, some as a potter as well. Further investigation would show us not only that Exekias is among quite a small number of individuals who can be identified by a name we can safely assume was the real one, but also that we can also think in terms of groups of pots which can be associated with a single maker or a pair of individuals, even though we do not know what their real names were, and can only use a convenient label for them. Exekias signed some of his work, including this amphora, 'Exekias made and painted me'. This is the origin of our assumption that in this case the maker was an experienced craftsman who, on the surviving evidence, reached what is often an extremely sophisticated standard of output, both as a manufacturer of the vessels themselves, and also as a technically clever and visually subtle painter. That said, despite the signature in this particular case, the whole body of work attributed to him is judged by other criteria, which we also use in the case of the majority of Greek painted pots, which bear no signature at all, but can be seen to have equally distinctive signs of a particular maker at work.

Athenian pottery of the sixth and fifth centuries BC, and its painters, are usually treated as the most distinctive and rewarding to study, and in some ways that is true, not least because they have been the most intensely studied already. This is where we begin to move back towards treating them as art, and looking at them in an art-historical way.

## Beazley and his attribution methods

During the nineteenth century, which was a period in which many areas of study were beginning to take on the methods and aims we now take for granted, scholars began to try to date the many vases in museum and other collections, to read the occasional inscriptions and signatures on them, and to try to attribute them to specific artists, as well as to try to explain the pictures, not always mythological, which appear on them.

The foundations of all these studies were laid in this period, not least in Germany, but they came together in the person of Sir John Beazley, who was born in Glasgow in 1885, and died in Oxford as an emeritus professor of that University in 1970. It is not too much of an exaggeration to claim that he was the creator, virtually single-handed, of modern vase-studies, and although many scholars are now beginning to feel that there may be less desirable consequences of his work, nothing that we now do could be done without what he achieved.

When Beazley started work on Athenian black- and red-figure vases, he was essentially confronted with a situation in which there were literally tens of thousands of these vases stored in museums and being excavated virtually daily, and no real system for understanding or classifying them. Beazley, helped by a phenomenal photographic memory, an outstanding eye, a rigorous filing system and a devoted wife, simply set out to devise one. One of his earliest publications was about the artist we now call the Berlin Painter, and he is, as it happens, one of the clearest hands to use to demonstrate how Beazley worked. He began at a time when art critics and dealers were beginning to dominate the art market, and to want to attribute unsigned paintings and statues to artists who were already known, or to invent conventional names for artists who did not sign their work, but who could be recognised as the producers of distinctive bodies of work by their style. People who did this used various methods, but one of the most influential was one invented rather earlier by Giuseppe Morelli, and this was adopted by Beazley, and his friend and supporter A.D. Trendall, who developed the same methods for work on South Italian pottery. It depends on the idea that a painter's drawing style is as distinctive and personal and consistent (though it develops over time) as our handwriting, and this means that a particular hand can be recognised whenever it appears, because it always draws some things in the same way.

The Berlin Painter is one of the easiest with whom to demonstrate this (see Fig. 14, overleaf). Among the more distinctive details of this drawing, the features which the Morelli-Beazley system will use are the left ankle bone, the right knee-cap, the extension of the pectorals over onto the upper arm, the hands, the shape of the head and its proportions. We should then be able to find the same details repeated in other drawings, for example Fig. 15 (on p. 37).

This painting of a kithara player shows the same treatment of the ankles and the hands, and the same small ear. The complex scene from the painter's so-called name vase, in Berlin (Fig. 16, on p. 38), has figures which demonstrate a combination of the same treatments of the anatomical details of its figures.

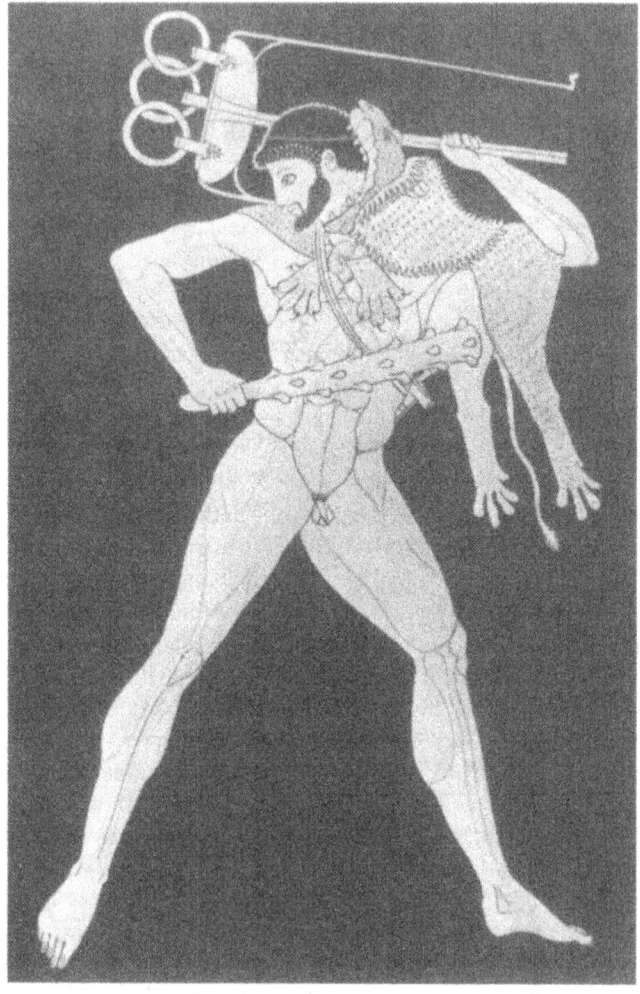

Fig. 14. Herakles with the tripod. Detail of an Attic red-figure amphora painted by the Berlin Painter. *c.* 500 BC. Martin von Wagner Museum. Würzburg.

Now this is comparatively easy: but Beazley also distinguished the Berlin Painter from his contemporary, the Kleophrades Painter (Fig. 17, on p. 39) from an earlier generation of painters, including Euthymides (Fig. 22) who taught them both, and from a probable pupil, and he did this with literally thousands of painters, both black- and red-figure. So he built up a picture of the way in which the Athenian pottery industry worked, and styles developed, about the relations of potters and painters to each

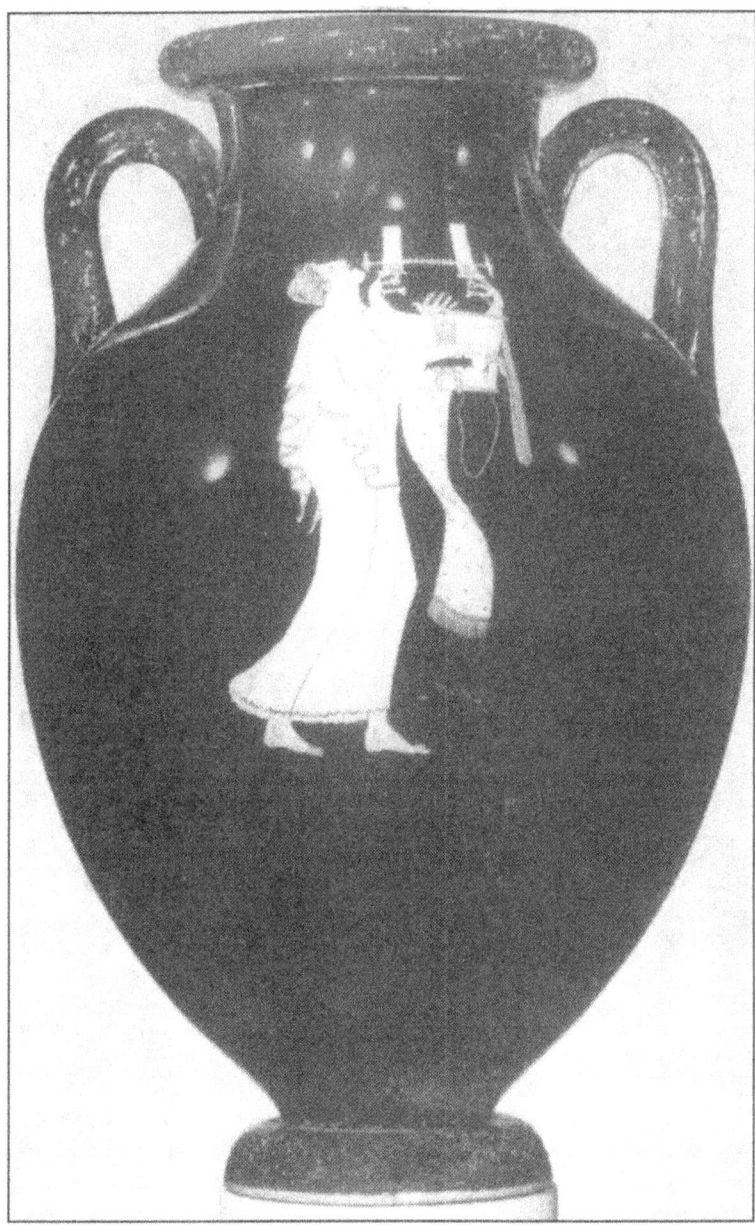

Fig. 15. Kithara player. Detail of an Attic red-figure amphora painted by the Berlin Painter. c. 500 BC. Metropolitan Museum of Art. New York. H. 41.5 cm.

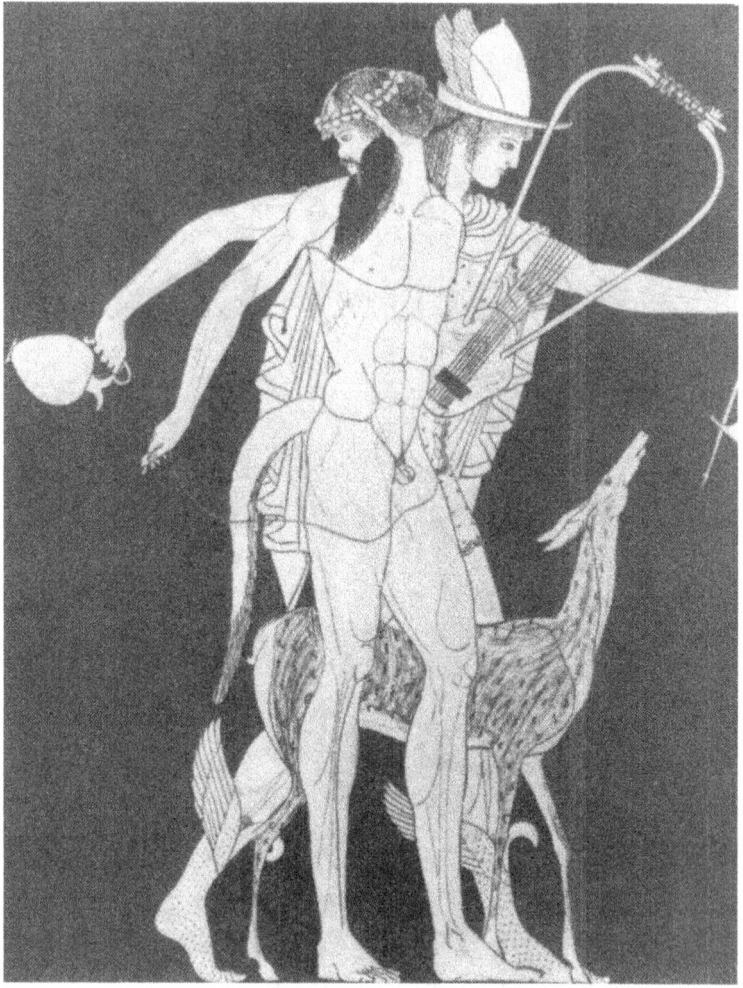

Fig. 16. Hermes and a satyr. Detail of an Attic red-figure amphora painted by the Berlin Painter. *c.* 500 BC. Staatliche Museen. Berlin.

other and to their customers and public, and laid down a chronological scheme, which, with certain reservations, is still the one used both by art-historians and by archaeologists whose major interest is in dates. What is more, these methods can be used, with modifications, for other local styles.

Like all great theorists, Beazley is beginning to have his detractors: objections have been raised to his picture of the Athenian pottery industry, on the grounds that it is too like the Arts and Crafts movement of Beazley's

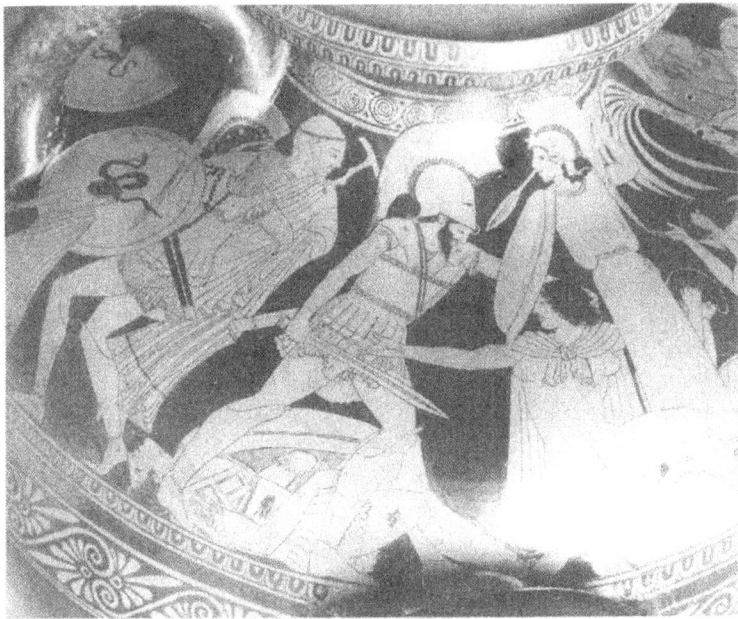

Fig. 17. Sack of Troy. Ajax and Kassandra. Detail of an Attic red-figure hydria painted by the Kleophrades Painter, c. 500-480 BC. Museo Archeologico, Naples.

own youth, or too like what is known about the Renaissance apprenticeship system, or simply that it seems too cut and dried, too cosy, too positivist for these negative times, or simply too difficult for others to practise, especially since Beazley shared his results, but not enough of his methods.

There has been considerable discussion since 1970 of Beazley's legacy, both in terms of his assumptions and his methods, and at least one serious, though now largely discredited, attempt to overturn the underlying chronological framework on which his view of the Athenian pottery industry rests. At worst, it could be argued with some truth that the life and career structure envisaged for Beazley's named painters is crude. It was supported by an approach to the body of material which presupposes, as its core assumption, that all such material is subject, as the product of human effort, to a gradual and measurable rise to a peak in quality, a productive plateau, and an equally gradual decline, over a working life of about 30 years. This pattern of production can be seen to be the output of progression from learner to teacher/practitioner to long-past-peak emeritus in the learning and skills curve of an identifiable individual. If we can make that skills curve equate to a chronology with an early, middle and late structure, then we can elaborate it to support all the other things we want to do with our material. Conversely, if we try to abandon it wholesale, as some have tried to, then in fact we have lost a useful mode of controlling a huge body of evidence for all kinds of things, as well as losing touch with an accepted, and better still, well-understood mode of understanding the human past and its products. In the contemporary context of approaches to archaeological study which concentrate on the human context and meaning of material objects, a view of painted Greek pottery which treats the development of its makers as fundamental is to be supported.

The overview in Chapter 1 of the chronological framework within which we situate Greek pottery used a few examples to show a progression from the stylised Geometric vessels of the post-Bronze age period to the highly sophisticated red-figure of Athens and the Greek cities of Southern Italy in the fifth to third centuries BC. That overview depends on the same sense that stylistic change can be mapped as a start from relatively simple beginnings, through a peak of achievement which reflects very high technical skill and aesthetic judgement, to a mature style which sits easily with the skills and taste which underpin it, and may easily tip over the edge into a decline when its practitioners become over-confident, lazy, or bored, or have refined their capabilities to a point where they are in a position to develop their practice. This last stage is that which generates stylistic change.

## Five case studies, five painters

Here we are going to look in detail at five amphorae, made at dates spread across four centuries by our chronological framework, but each characteristic of its period and of its painter. In this way we shall also be able to look at the changes in shape, size and function of one particular type of pot over time, and also at the characteristics we look for when attributing a group of work to a painter, and the development of painting techniques and skills in our period. We met some of them briefly in the chronological survey in Chapter 1.

We saw that Athens 804 (Fig. 18), the large burial amphora showing a funeral, is often illustrated as the starting point in the developmental pattern, both chronologically and in terms of Athenian practitioners' mastery of the potter's craft. The amphora is roughly 1.55 m in height, which makes it extremely large and, from the potter's viewpoint, a considerable technical achievement in its own right. The local iron-rich clay provides a dense, strong fabric which allows for the construction of

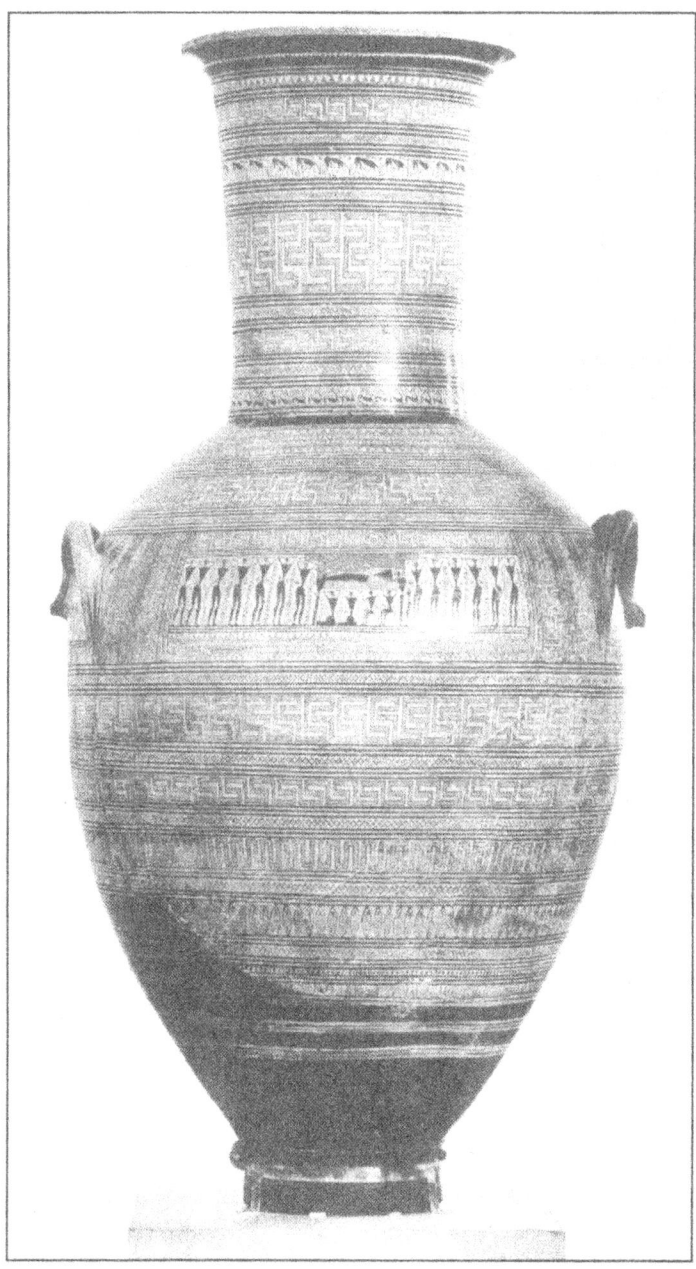

Fig. 18. Athens 804. Attic geometric amphora painted by the Dipylon Painter,
mid-eighth century BC. National Archaeological Museum, Athens. H. 1.55 m.

the vessel from several components. The natural properties of the clay also allow it to be diluted to form the glaze-paint used to decorate it, and a multi-stage firing process produces the black patterns or figures on the red background. This technique will aid later styles of painting too.

The painter created a controlled pattern of ribbon-like bands covering the pot with a variegated two-colour texture. It has been suggested that the inspiration for this kind of decorative treatment may have been textiles; it is possible that the repeated woven structures of basketry play their part too. It is important to notice the way in which the width of the bands varies with the shape of the pot, following its swelling curve, and narrowing again. The neck carries the most extended version of the maeander pattern, and it also carries two ribbons of grazing deer and goats. These repeat the single stylised animal as a continuous procession around the vessel. The lower band marks the join between the neck and the body of the pot, the upper emphasises the widening mouth.

The position of the handles at the curve of the shoulder provides the major point of emphasis, which is reinforced by the appearance of the funeral picture between them. It is made to stand out in the overall texture by the vertical elements of its frame, and the echoing verticals of the standing and seated figures. Not only does the picture have a frame, which positions it at the beginning of the European tradition of representations in a defined picture space, but it also concentrates the viewer's attention on the purpose of the pot, at the point at which his or her eye will most readily focus.

The picture itself presents part of the funeral ceremony as a single freeze-frame, in which thirteen adult mourners and a child are disposed on either side of the central bier, on which the deceased woman lies, exposed artificially to view by the lifting of her chequered shroud. Four other mourners are shown in front of the bier, two seated on stools, two kneeling. The figures are stylised in the same way as the animals –

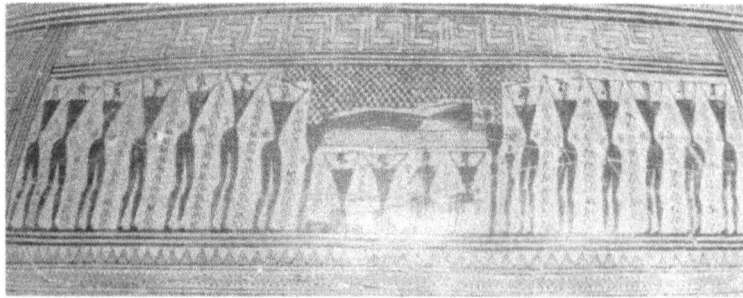

Fig. 19. Athens 804, detail.

articulated by the essential joints so that they take on much the same emphasis on structure as the vessel itself does. The heads are a tear-drop blob, the torso and arms a triangle, with which the precise curvatures of hips and legs contrast sharply. Between the figures are columns of zig-zags, sometimes read as stylised foliage, representing funeral wreaths. All these characteristic elements of the picture, and its figures, can be found in other, related, funeral pictures; the ones showing male burials extend the same principles of stylisation to chariot processions and horses. This allows us to see that a single painter with a recognisable style was at work, producing grave markers for elite burials in a group grave-plot in an important Athenian cemetery. It also suggests that we have a body of work centred on a group of commissions from a workshop which catered for a specialised demand for a particular type of vessel, perhaps from a group of related patrons, for a highly specific purpose.

The vessel itself, with other comparable examples, fits into our chrono-logical structure both as a peak in the development of the Geometric style of Greek vase painting, and as an ancestor of later treatments of its subject-matter and of the relationship between shape and decoration that it displays. It is dated to around 750 BC, and already has many of the characteristics we study in the later black- and red-figure pots of archaic and classical Athens.

A style as distinctive as this one can sustain itself only for a limited period; this particular style has clear limitations for the painter. It may be possible to use it to tell less generic stories, but before long, its lack of opportunity for individual treatment of character or event means that the painter will seek a more flexible mode of expression. The interest in the human figure engaged in an activity which may become part of a narrative is established, but the painter will need other kinds of tool to develop true narrative art. A few Geometric representations of battles, shipwrecks, and even a hero fighting a lion (see Fig. 31), show that the impetus to get beyond the functional funeral representation was there.

By the latter half of the eighth century BC innovative painters were beginning to emphasise the figures more, and to use animals and monsters, probably inspired by figurative textiles and objects from the Near East. Representations of heroes engaged in combat, occasionally with animals, become more commonplace, and by the middle of the seventh century, styles of painting in the major Greek cities became more visibly exuber-ant, experimental, and much more evidently geared towards storytelling. We should note that this is also the period at which the *Iliad* and the *Odyssey* in some form were in circulation as oral poetry; heroic story-telling which was to remain an major influence on Greek culture was taking shape in verbal form, to which we can see the development of narrative art as a visual parallel in an intensely visual culture. The Eleusis amphora (Fig. 20), like Athens 804, did duty as a grave marker, and indeed as a burial vessel. It, too, is an outsize two-handled jar, with a tall flaring neck. Although it retains some animal decoration, its emphasis is on the two figure scenes on its neck and belly. It dates from a little before the middle of the seventh century BC, and the striking treatment of one of its major scenes inspired the conventional name for its author: this is the name vase of the Polyphemus Painter. He is also credited with a number of other striking works, among them a stand with a row of marching warriors including Menelaus, who is labelled, and a now fragmentary krater which may show Cheiron, Achilles' centaur tutor. Our amphora shows one of the most dramatic and memorable episodes from the story of Odysseus, the blinding of the one-eyed cannibal giant Polyphemus; the body has an early chase episode – the Gorgons pursuing Perseus, who has cut off their sister Medusa's head and carried it off. On the upper shoulder is a panel containing a lion attacking a boar. There is a wide variety of pattern, both framing bands and a scatter of filling motifs, but the emphasis is now very much on the narrative pictures rather than overall pattern, and the bold, curving, even rubbery figures are the eye-catchers.

The neck picture shows the work of a painter who used his picture space to advantage. If Polyphemus is to be a giant by comparison with Odysseus and his party, and they are to be given significant size, he will have to be fitted into the picture by sitting him down. This can also be used to suggest that he is sleepy and partially incapacitated by drink, and the wine-cup he holds suggests that too. He leans against the picture frame, and tries to brush Odysseus' blinding stake away. Odysseus and his companions form a series of tall verticals across the picture, and Odysseus himself is given an outline body, originally painted white, to contrast with his companions, who are silhouettes apart from the outline face given to all the figures. The way in which the heads are drawn is one of the identifiers which appears again in other work attributed to this painter, with their long vertical axis and domed skull shape. The particular mixture of outline and silhouette is another, and the figures on the Menelaus stand show these clearly, along with the elongated body proportions, and the choice of filling ornament.

The body frieze uses the absence of handles on the body to show the Gorgons chasing Perseus away from their collapsing and decapitated sister Medusa. Perseus, another elongated, slightly rubbery silhouette, disappears round the side of the vessel, protected by an outline Athena

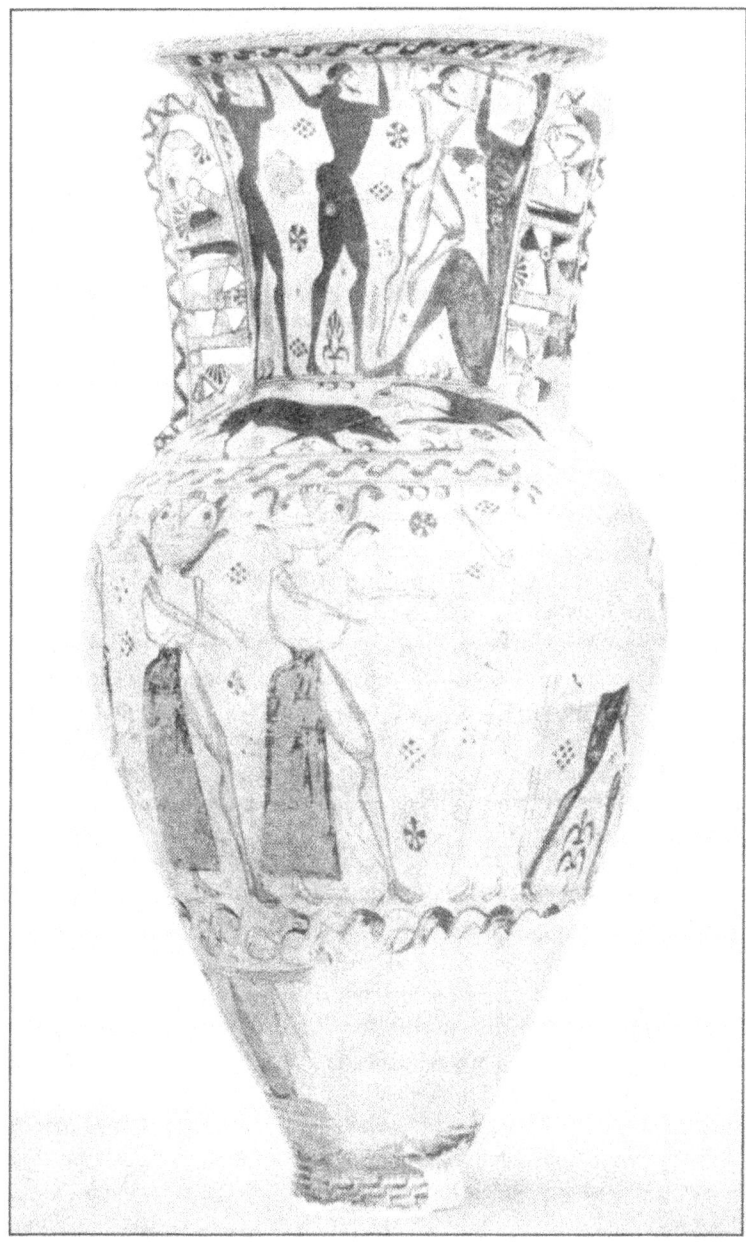

Fig. 20. Odysseus and Polyphemus: Gorgons. Attic amphora painted by the Polyphemus Painter, mid-seventh century BC. Eleusis Museum, Eleusis. H. 1.42 m.

from his pursuers. Gorgons turn their adversaries to stone with a glance; the inference is that their faces are particularly horrific. Later on they become standardised with a frontal lion-like mask, but the painter had at this stage no prototypes for what a Gorgon should look like, and what we see is a pair of creatures with a human body and a head which seems to be derived from a metal cauldron with snaky attachments – in fact a type of cauldron of which there are surviving examples from this period. The heads are made to coincide with the most prominent part of the body of the vase, so that our eye meets them first; this is yet another example of a design-sensibility which considers the relationship between the picture and its pot very seriously, as is the chase as a subject for a vessel which the viewer can walk around, beginning to look at it at any point. This is also true of the Polyphemus Painter's Menelaus stand, where he used a procession in the same way.

Our Ajax and Achilles amphora (see Figs 1, 34) is usually dated to around 540-530 BC, a little more than a century later than our previous example. By this time the decorated amphora is more usually of a domestic size; this one is 61 cm high. It is painted in a fully evolved black-figure technique, and the shape, known as Type A, is one of the standard types used in Athens at this point. It may have been invented or at least refined by Exekias himself. It is potted in a continuous curve, with flanged handles bearing an ivy trail on the vertical face, and a stepped foot. This example displays its pictures in the way which become standard for this shape, and they appear in a panel between the handles on either side, with a band of pattern at the top. Sometimes the pictures are related in subject, as is probably the case here, but often they are not, and then there is clearly an A-side, with the more original or complex picture, and a B-side with a much more generic and occasionally less carefully-painted scene. Notice that the position of the picture is carefully related to the widest part of the pot, and the position of the handles.

In this particular case, the composition of the picture illustrated in Fig. 1 is designed to relate to the handles too – the viewer's eye is led by the warriors' spears upwards via the upper handle-root around the flange and down to their stacked armour. Once again their heads are on the outward curve of the belly of the pot. The warriors and their spears form a pair of interwoven triangles, their heads at the apex of one, the spears making another, and we can find several other subsidiary triangles and lozenges if we look. The detailed incised textures of their cloaks and hair, the large arched eye-shape, and bold, slightly pointed facial profile are all charac-teristics of this painter. So is the distribution of patterned and black areas across the image, and the way the two large figures are disposed to emphasise them against their red background, and to avoid confusing overlaps which would detract from the clarity of the scene.

The other side of the amphora (Fig. 34) shows a family gathered to see off – or perhaps welcome home – one of the sons of the house. The occasion is ambiguous, perhaps deliberately, but we see one of the sons with the family dog, mother, the second son with his horse, whose nose is being patted by father. He is accompanied by a small boy carrying a stool, a folded garment, and an aryballos with oil, the standard signs of a bath. This painting shows the same figure and face types, with the same meticulous attention to detail in the way in which textiles and hair are incised. Here, the son with the horse is framed by the other figures; the son with the dog and the father bend with the curvature of the pot itself.

On both sides of the vessel the figures are labelled, so that we know that the gaming warriors are Ajax and Achilles, and the family on the other side are Kastor and Polydeukes and their mother and stepfather, Leda and Tyndareus. Exekias also signed the vessel, and provided inscriptions for Ajax and Achilles which act as speech balloons and tell us what their scores are – Achilles is winning, with four, and Ajax, as his bent head perhaps implies, losing, with three. The inscriptions are as characteristically neat and controlled as the figures, and the total effect of both pictures is striking, dramatic and intense. It is not accidental that the Ajax and Achilles side is one of the most illustrated of all Greek vase paintings, and is often treated as the high point of the style.

Exekias, like other black-figure painters, used added red and white, extra colours painted on after firing. He tended to be sparing of his added colours, and they are usually accents which supply emphasis. Achilles' dominant helmet has a red crest, and he is wearing a red headband under it, echoed by a similar one round Ajax's head. Both have a red chiton, and the satyr mask on Achilles' shield is red too. Their corselets are white. On the other side, red is used for Castor's cloak, Leda's dress, and the folded cloak on the stool, and the dog was once white, as was Leda's flesh.

Black-figure, like the Geometric style, can be extraordinarily sophisticated and dramatic, but it is one which has limitations for the painter who aims for any kind of realism, or for drawing which will allow exploration of the human body, or the suggestion of three-dimensionality on a flat surface. We see objects and people, whatever their colour, as an assembly of highlights and recessions, related to other objects and backgrounds by distance from each other and from the viewer. Modern techniques for suggesting this spatial relationship in a two-dimensional medium play with colour gradation and the relative sizes of figures or objects, so that those which are further away are smaller and darker than those at the front. A medium which uses only two major colours will present the would-be realistic painter with obvious difficulties; black-figure, using silhouettes, works against suggestions of depth and makes it hard to overlap or entwine figures without obscuring their actions.

In the last thirty years of the sixth century BC, Greek sculptors began to use bronze as well as marble, and at the same time to show a greater tendency towards anatomically accurate figures. Their vase-painting contemporaries in Athens began to show a similar interest in the structure of the human body, and they evolved a style in which it was easier to do it. Red-figure began as a reversal of black-figure, with the figures as line drawings on the red surface of the clay, surrounded by a black background. At the start, the balance of light and dark areas of the picture, and even the drawing style, is not very different, but fifth-century red-figure progresses via experiments with foreshortening, and eventually a more variable density of line, and a more fluid and sketchy drawing style, towards a technique which is recognisably the ancestor of modern European drawing.

The amphora illustrated in Fig. 21, one side in black-figure, one side in red-figure, was probably painted by the same artist, the Andokides Painter, on both sides, though some scholars prefer to think that he did the red-figure side, and a partner known to us as the Lysippides Painter was responsible for the black-figure picture. Both show Herakles at a feast, attended by Athena; the black-figure side includes Hermes, a servant, and a dinos on a stand. It was painted in the late sixth century, and is characteristic of the so-called bilingual pieces which illustrate the change of painting technique from black-figure to red-figure. It is in the same size-range as the Exekian one, and amphorae do not vary very much in size from now on.

The black-figure side has Herakles, wearing an elaborately striped and dotted himation over his legs, propped up on his elbow against a cushion on his kline, holding a kantharos. Athena, wearing an equally elaborately patterned peplos and her snake-fringed aegis, holds her spear at a slant in her left hand, and extends her right to greet Herakles. At the extreme left of the picture is Hermes, wearing his hat and boots and a striped cloak; the servant, who is naked, dips into the dinos at the right. Beyond them all is a vine with grapes, in which hangs Herakles' bow and quiver; before the kline is a table with loaves, strips of meat, a plate of figs, and a kylix. Athena's aegis and Herakles' hair are represented by fine incised textures, and the textiles, furniture mounts, and the vine all contribute to the sense of detail and pattern. There are no large expanses of unfilled space, and an even balance between the dark, light and patterned areas of the picture.

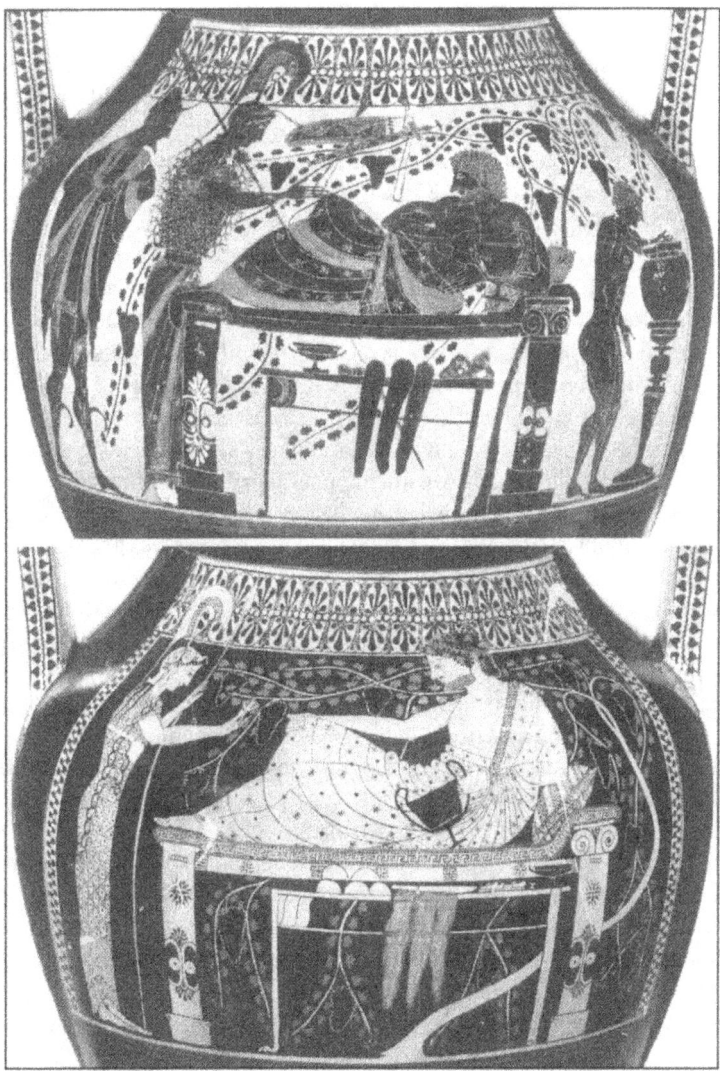

Fig. 21. Herakles feasted by Athena. Detail of an Attic bilingual amphora painted by the Andokides Painter. c. 530-515 BC. Staatliche Antikensammlungen und Glyptothek. Munich.

The figures and furniture stand on the same ground line, and any sense of differential distance from the viewer is achieved by overlap. Athena's helmet and spear-head, and Hermes' hat protrude into the framing pattern at the top of the scene, and the natural reading for us is to view them as being in front of it. This painter, like some others of around this date, makes occasional attempts to suggest space outside the picture frame in this way. Herakles is posed with profile legs and head, and a frontal chest, with incised collarbones, pectorals, and upper-arm muscles. These details are not common in mature black-figure, but begin to appear more frequently once red-figure appears too: they are the kind of detail which a line-drawing technique uses naturally. The slightly awkward mixture of frontal and profile aspects of the body is also extremely typical of the gradual move from the essentially profile silhouettes of black-figure towards the convincing three-quarter views of mature red-figure. Equally typical is the filled and busy picture space, with no big gaps between figures and objects, and the presence of the tree as part of the fill.

The red-figure side is not an exact reversal of the black-figure one, though some other examples of bilingual amphorae attributed to this painter, or pair of painters, do equate the two sides more closely. Instead, though the subject of the scene is the same, the feast involves just Herakles and his patron Athena. Herakles is once again displayed on a kline in front of a vine, this time without his weapons hanging in it. The painter has missed the section of the vine-trunk which should appear between the leg of the table at the right, and the leg of the kline near it. This is an easy mistake, because the two colours of clay are very similar before firing; the painter exhibits a difficulty with narrow shapes outlined by the black glaze, such as outstretched fingers, for the same technical reason. Before Herakles is the same table with the same feast, slightly differently arranged upon it. The kylix is painted in black-figure. Herakles and his kline are now larger in relation to the rest of the scene, and his head and Athena's helmet crest both protrude into the top frame. The effect of this, together with the red-figure technique which highlights them, is to make both figures very prominent, and to suggest a separation from the picture-space. Herakles' posture is now slightly more upright, though still propped on the cushion, with his kantharos in hand. The painter drew his left leg, and the bent knee of his right one, exactly as he evidently did their black-figure equivalents, before he added the cloak draped over them, and the cloak appears transparent and patterned, with the legs visible through it. The painter showed Herakles' collar-bones on a frontal chest, and managed to articulate Herakles' hands, clasped round his kantharos-handle and his knee, with some conviction. His head is still in profile, and so is the complete figure of Athena, a tall figure at the edge of the picture. She wears an elaborately patterned and pleated dress under the aegis, and a tall helmet with a stilted crest, as on the black-figure side. She grasps an upright spear, and holds out a flower in her other hand towards Herakles – a gesture of welcome which matches that made by Leda on Exekias' amphora. The Andokides Painter's work shows a number of characteristic habits, including the distribution of patterned and plain areas in his compositions, which relate to the work of Exekias in this way, and Beazley suggested that the Andokides Painter was Exekias' pupil, training, naturally, as a black-figure painter. He may have invented red-figure, of which the work attributed to him is among the earliest surviving examples. There are other groups of painters whose work exhibits related stylistic features, suggesting shared training and a shared teacher in the same way.

Both scenes appear within a patterned frame. The patterns on both sides of the vase are black-figure: red-figure ones develop a little later, particularly in the work of cup painters. Both scenes show a lotus and palmette chain, one of the most standard of all Athenian framing motifs, across the top; the red-figure side has vertical dotted zigzags at the sides too, where the black-figure side has a plain line at each side. On both sides, the ground line on which the figures stand is black, with a red space below it. Both sides show some added red for clothing details, and the red-figure side uses it for the strips of meat on the table, the leaves on the vine, Herakles' beard, and the leaves of the wreath in his hair. On the black-figure side white is used for Athena's flesh, as is usual in this technique, and for furniture mounts and the dotted patterns on clothing. The colour and patterns provide accent and variety, and it was a while before red-figure painters abandoned the black-figure habits of surface texture and colour, and the packed composition of their pictures. The overall effect, if not the detail, of these two scenes, is very similar.

A taste for scenes which show off the human figure goes in hand with the added capacity provided by the red-figure technique to show its anatomical structure. Where black-figure tended to rely on the convention of mixing profile and frontal views, red-figure painters of what Beazley regarded as the second generation began to exploit their line drawing capacity to suggest three-dimensionality and views of the body which are neither fully frontal nor fully profile. Selective detail and greater control of the contour of the figure help the illusion. Euthymides, the painter responsible for the red-figure amphora (Fig. 22, overleaf) showing three men dancing after a party, was a member of a group of related painters, labelled the Pioneer Group by Beazley. They may all have been pupils of the Andokides Painter, to whom their work can be related stylistically; they inscribed their vases with messages to each other which suggest a close awareness of each other's work.

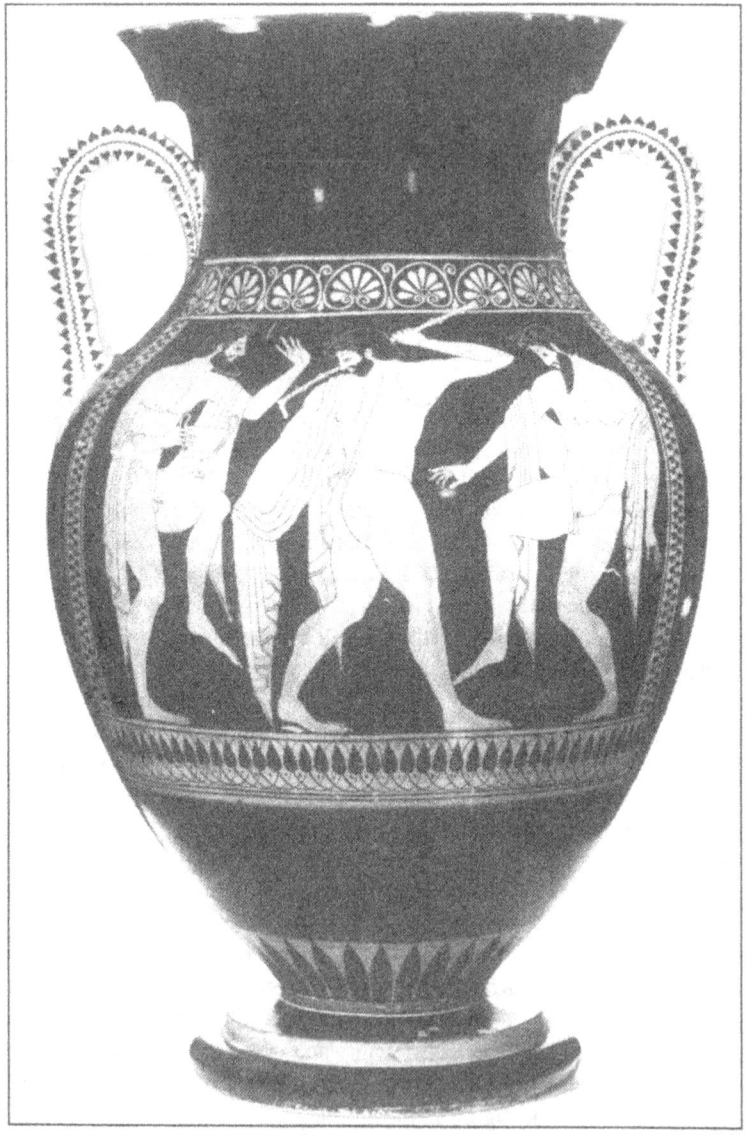

Fig. 22. Komos. Attic red-figure amphora painted by Euthymides. *c.* 510-500 BC.
Staatliche Antikensammlungen und Glyptothek. Munich. H. 60.3 cm.

This amphora displays the revellers in the traditional panel, the two framing figures once again shaped and positioned to fit the curvature of the vessel. They are shown frontally, and they draw attention to the very fine three-quarter back view of the central man. The painter realised that if the shoulder blades were shaped differently, and the line of the spine curved diagonally from the neck towards the profile buttocks, the figure could be made to appear to twist at the waist. The figure is achieved with great economy of detail and a neat control of its outer contour. The painter challenged his colleague Euphronios, also a painter with an interest in anatomy and three-dimensional suggestion, in an inscription at the side of the scene – 'Euphronios never did this!' The sharp-eyed faces and slightly meaty bodies of his three men are among the distinguishing characteristics which appear elsewhere in this painter's work.

The three men wear red-leaved party wreaths, but otherwise the scene concentrates on the figures, with little interest in pattern. The handles exhibit the black-figure ivy-trail, and the side and bottom frames of the show the dotted zigzag and a lotus-bud interlace, another common black-figure band-pattern. The top frame, however, has a red-figure band of palmettes and tendrils; versions of this, of varying degrees of elaboration, continue to appear throughout the fifth century.

All five amphorae discussed here are characteristic both of their period and their style; all five allow for exploration of the techniques of their painters; all five can be related to other work by the same hands. Beazley's attribution methods demonstrated that a signature is not necessary to allow us to identify the hand, at least as one recognisable in a body of work, and that we can think about makers with distinctive artistic personalities and interests.

# Chapter 3

## Shapes and their Uses

Our Ajax and Achilles amphora (Fig. 1) is an example of a type of two-handled wine jar which is a standard shape used by Athenian vase painters as one of the more convenient forms to which to apply their pictures. A significant part of its importance to us is that it is one of thousands of surviving examples of a common shape which changed gradually over two to three centuries, gradually displaying altered proportions, experiments with handle shapes, and especially different concepts of the right way to decorate it. Almost all the other common shapes of Greek painted pottery display the same evolutionary development: this is one of the major factors supporting our ability to date them, or at least to arrange them in a consistent series, which can then provide relative dates. It is often possible to relate one or more stages in the developmental series to a real date, by one of the methods discussed in Chapter 1.

Our amphora is just one of a number of standard vessel shapes associated with particular occasions and uses, all of which reflect domestic and formal or religious concerns. Broadly speaking, the larger container shapes, especially amphorae, appear as relatively big examples in the Geometric period, and moderate in size and shape to the needs of domestic use as opposed to the commemorative marker over the next two centuries. A process of gradual refinement usually means that the later versions of the shape may have exaggeratedly elongated narrow contours, where the mid-term version of the late archaic and early classical period may well be the most stable and practical stage of the development. The smaller shapes, designed for frequent handling in daily use, often change less, and undergo very slight adjustments. They often travel virtually unchanged across local fabrics too.

The changes which a particular shape can undergo over three or four centuries allow, as we have seen, for relative dating; in a smaller timeframe we can see experiments, and occasionally the work of a particular potter undergoing evolution as his taste and skills move on. Our amphora belongs in the middle of a process of development in which the shape itself started with a wider body than ours has, and could have several different types of handle, mouth or foot. The mouth of our amphora is angled, the foot has a step with a concave upper surface and a second, curved member, and the handles are essentially a ribbon with vertical flanges. On another amphora the mouth may be rolled, and so may its single-member foot; the handles might be rolled and so round or ovoid in section rather than flat. In essence, a particular shape usually becomes more streamlined as it matures, though it will usually retain the major characteristics which make it what it is, with some vestiges of a relationship with its original practical use; more flamboyant shapes tend to be later, and to carry equally flamboyant decoration. Tastes change, both in drawing style, and in the articulation of the decoration with the vase shape; the format of the pictures is as important as their content.

The shape chart (Fig. 23, overleaf) shows us outlines of the sixth- and fifth-century BC versions of most of the common vessels in use in Athens in the late Archaic and Classical periods. In their turn, these vessel types stand for a much wider set of variants on shapes designed for a set of core functions, for which we tend to use a standard set of names. These are well established by custom and practice over the last 150 years; we cannot be sure that all of them correspond with the names used by the Greeks themselves. They include containers, or so-called closed shapes, and cups and bowls, or open shapes. Some of them are sophisticated versions of functional storage jars; the latter were often on a larger scale than the decorated examples, and were used as trade containers as well as larder jars; others were mainly produced for special or specialised occasions, and their decoration relates them to their intended function: a funerary vessel may show a funeral, and a formal wine vessel a wine-related myth or a picture of a drinking party. The idea of using a well-understood and familiar type of vessel, and fitting it to a special purpose by the use of particular types of decoration, is extremely common in ancient Greek culture; it can be paralleled by the equally frequent habit of using a generic scene, but populating it with characters from heroic legend.

There are a few shapes which would nowadays be made in other materials, at any rate for practical use; the *pyxis*, which is a box, varies in size and may be a pillbox shape, as our shape chart shows it, or may look more like a spool or cotton-reel. Sometimes it is shaped like a modern cardboard talcum-powder drum, with a drop-over lid. We would often use paper or plastics to make a box of this type; in their absence, the ancient Greek potter made his storage for scented solids, jewellery and other small objects from a fine ceramic, and it was often buried with its owner and user, or specifically created to stand for the domestic values its decoration represents in a burial group.

Our shape-chart is arranged in the way in which it appears here for a

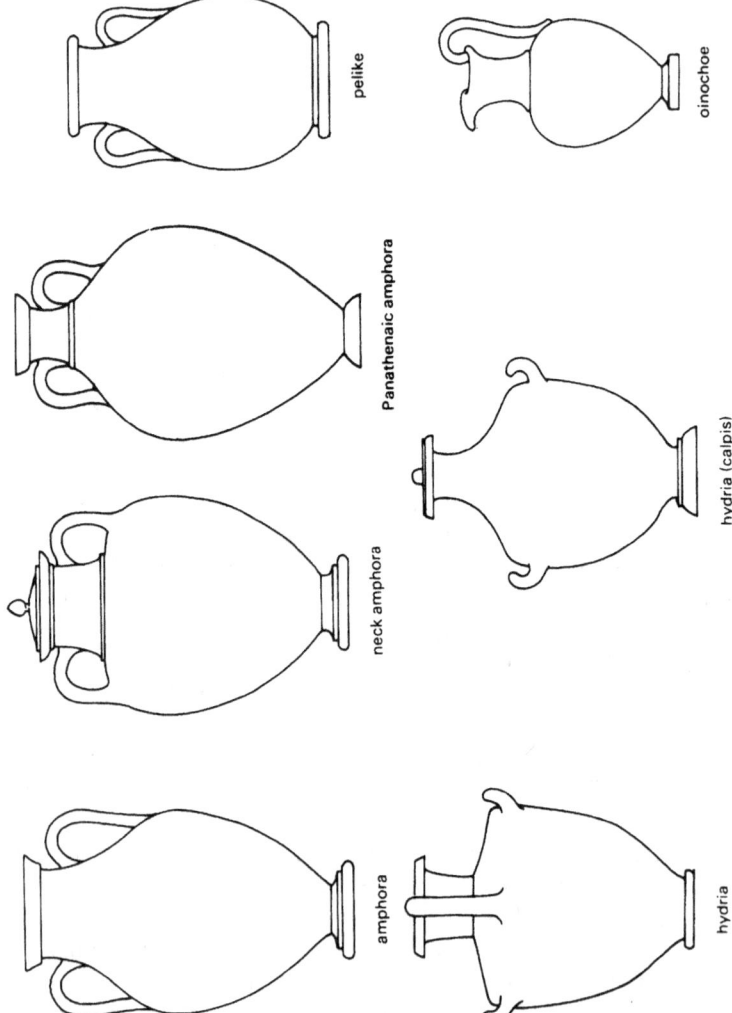

pelike

oinochoe

Panathenaic amphora

neck amphora

hydria (calpis)

amphora

hydria

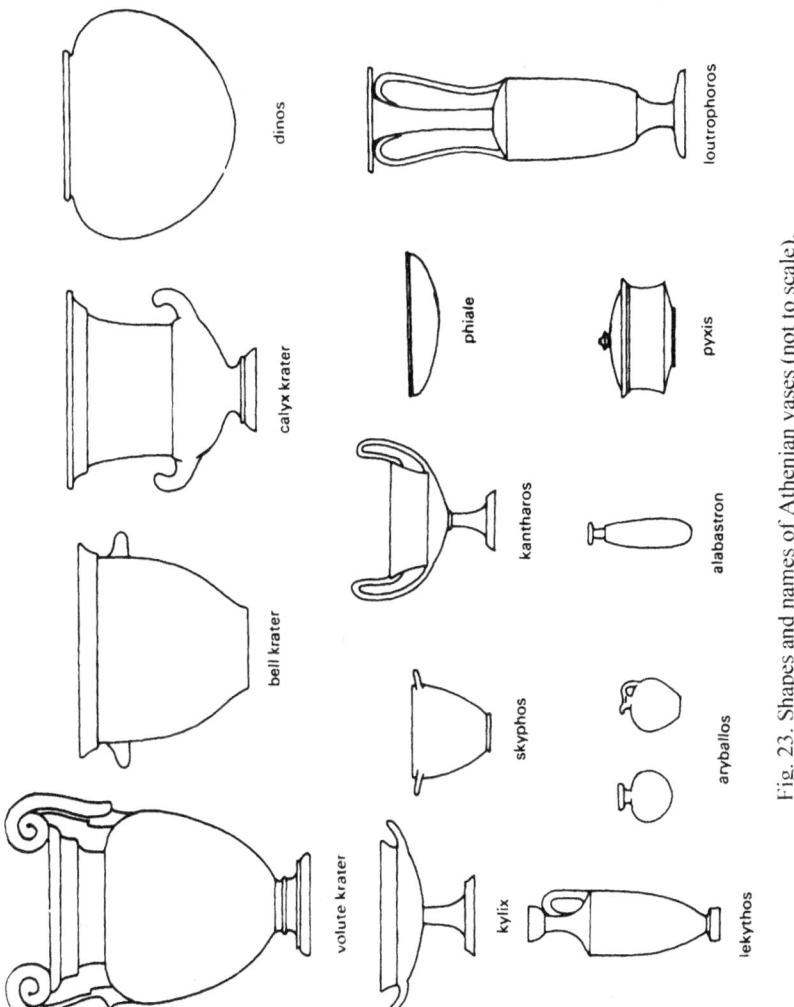

Fig. 23. Shapes and names of Athenian vases (not to scale).

reason: the vessel groups largely correspond to the uses of decorated vases to contain or dispense the three major fluids which appear in use throughout ancient Mediterranean society, both domestically and ritually. They also correspond with the way in which the vessels actually work functionally. The top row of jars are mainly containers for wine, three of them related in shape to commercial transport amphorae designed for stacking head to tail, as we would bottles, in the hold of a ship or on a cart. The commercial ones usually come to a point at the foot, and were held upright, if necessary, in a roughly-potted stand, some of which survive; the formal ones have an integral base, and stand alone. The first two amphora-shapes (see also Figs 1, 7, 8, 22) show vessels with a relatively wide mouth; they could be used for formal presentation of solids as well as liquids, and so could the *pelike*.

The *Panathenaic amphora* has a narrow neck, an indicator of its use as an oil jar; in fact it is another variant on the commercial shape, which was always differentiated from the wine containers both by the sharp taper to its upper and lower contours and by its decoration; it was the container for oil awarded as a prize in the Panathenaic Games, a major athletic event in the Athenian calendar. It carried a picture of the event for which the prize was awarded on one side, and a picture of Athena, with commemorative inscriptions, on the other. The evidence suggests that winners were awarded a large number of these containers as a single prize: their contents represented a considerable capital asset, and they could sell them on. The property of Alcibiades and others accused of desecrating the Herms in 415 was auctioned in the aftermath, and included over 100 Panathenaics which changed hands for around half a drachma each. Their decoration remained in the black-figure style throughout, long after it had gone out of use for other purposes.

Olive oil of varying degrees of quality supplied the Greek world with lighting, a soap equivalent, scent, moisturiser, a cooking medium, a ritual unguent, and lubricants for multifarious purposes. Most of the other jars designed to contain it which appear in our chart are intended for smaller quantities, and in most cases to be portable. The *lekythos* was the medium-sized standard bottle (see Fig. 28), which, with appropriate decoration and variation in shape, held oil for the table, occasionally for baby oil, for rituals, especially those associated with the burial of the dead, and for offering and deposit at the grave. Those designed to fulfil this last function often carry a picture of visitors to a burial site marked by a gravestone on steps, on which lekythoi left by similar visitors stand. In the latter half of the fifth century they may not only have a scene painted on them related to their function, but may also be decorated in white-ground. This is a technique which first appears at the beginning of the fifth century as an alternative to the red background of black-figure vessels, and later develops as a way of introducing colour onto vase surfaces. The white slip cannot be fired, and is therefore fugitive; its use on funerary pottery which would not be handled regularly and subjected to wear and tear is a logical one.

The *aryballos*, usually, though not always, about the size of a clenched fist (see Fig. 4), is a small personal container for scented oil – in some ways a soap-on-a-rope or after-sun equivalent. We see representations on vases of it suspended by a cord from the wrist of its owner, or hung in a tree beside the fountain house in which he is having a shower. Occasionally he is shown turning it upside-down to shake the contents out onto his palm so that he can rub himself down with it. The flat mouth is designed to help the process. The decoration frequently relates to athletic or post-battle use.

The *alabastron* was a largely female scent bottle; the shape itself is a ceramic version of a type of bottle originally made of alabaster in Egypt; Greek pottery versions of it appear from the eighth century BC onwards; the shape in our chart, which is very close to its Egyptian prototype, first appears in Athens in the mid-sixth century BC, and may have been introduced by Amasis, a potter working in Athens, but possibly of Egyptian origin. Its ceramic version often carries pictures of activity specifically associated with women and their official household rôle, occasionally weddings, and sometimes myths associated with female deities or heroines.

The *hydria* is a formal version of a domestic jar used for fetching water from a communal source for the household. Undecorated versions which survive were presumably the normal vessels of daily use for visits to the well. The fine ones, often with pictures of a group of women fetching water from a fountain house, were designed for formal use, including, probably, the water mixed with wine in the symposium. The angled shape with a sharp shoulder is the earlier, late sixth-century shape; its flat shoulder and large body provide a painter with an opportunity for a frieze picture on the shoulder, and a large panel scene on the body. The *kalpis*, or curved shape (see Fig. 12), is a later, usually smaller vessel popular in the fifth century and decorated in red-figure, often most successfully with single figure or a closely integrated group in the centre front of the body, and a pattern on the down-turned lip.

The *loutrophoros* is a specialised ritual water jar, normally used in Athens to carry the water either for a bride's bath, or for the washing of a corpse in the early stages of a burial; the washing is an indicator of a rite of passage. The vessel itself can be formed as an amphora with two handles, or a hydria with two small horizontal lugs and a single vertical handle parallel with the neck. Normally the body carries a picture of the event for which it was designed; the shape evolves from an angular archaic shape to a more curvaceous fifth- and fourth-century version.

The *oinochoe* is a jug; its name means a wine pourer, and that was at least part of its function. Its shape varies – it often has a spout, but it may be more like a mug, with a round mouth. It also varies widely in size, from an elegant but unstable late shape with a tall offset stand and an ovoid body, to a miniature potted in a continuous curve, with a trefoil mouth. There is also a round-mouthed version which originated in Corinth and was popular in Athens in the last thirty years of the sixth century; its shape and capacity suggest that it may have been used more often as a mug.

The *krater* is a mixing bowl (see Figs 9, 10, 13, 25); its name comes from the Greek word for mixing, and its simpler shapes relate to all-purpose kitchen basins; the bell krater, in particular, is a smaller, smarter version of a common type called a *lekanis*, which did duty, in various sizes, as among other things, a bread and cake mixing bowl, a temporary container, and even, outside in the yard of the house, as a lavatory. The column krater was, as far as we know, originally a Corinthian vase; the columns of its name appear as the supports to the handle-plate; it appears as a formal Athenian shape in the mid-sixth century, and was evidently popular enough to survive in much the same form into the fourth. Some other shapes would work equally well or better in metal; the volute krater clearly is not well-designed to survive intact when made in clay: the high-swung curly handles are much more secure when cast in metal. We have some surviving metal examples, with wonderful cast figures bolted to the neck, where their ceramic counterparts, impressive, but undoubtedly cheaper, have painted friezes. The calyx krater is really a version of the kylix cup-shape, with its rim extended upwards to form a wide trumpet-shaped vessel. The upper part of the pot allows for a frieze or two sizeable panel pictures. If the servers at a symposium are ladling fluid out of it, this and the bell krater are the most practical: there is no incurved rim on which to catch the ladle and spill the contents.

The *kyathos* (Fig. 24) is just such a ladle; its ceramic version is an Athenian invention based on an Etruscan original which often was made in metal. The handle, like that of the related kantharos, is fragile and does not survive well if made of pottery. A good many kyathoi were clearly made by potters who recognised this, along with their clients, and they appear as white-ground versions for funerary use. The cup of the vessel is often extremely delicate and finely potted.

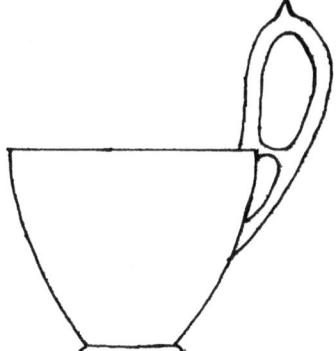

Fig. 24. Attic kyathos. *c.* 480 BC.

The term *dinos* implies turning or spinning (see Fig. 41); at least one authority on the shapes and names of Greek vases claims that this has no roots in antiquity, and Athenians contemporary with its manufacture would have called it a *lebes*, and equated it, like the bell krater, with other forms of domestic hollow-ware, many of them multifunctional. Be that as it may, it is different from the other lebes-shapes in one very obvious respect – it has a round bottom, where the others have a flat base; if it is to have any stability it will need a stand. Some surviving decorated examples, like that shown in Fig. 41, do have a matching stand made for them. And in this respect it is unlike the other formal krater shapes which all have integral stands supporting the bowl; the bell krater, which is nearer to the domestic basin, has a flat base. And unlike the other krater shapes a dinos usually has no handles. Its implications are ones of interaction with a group of people arranged round it, with a communal view of it and of each other. Many dinoi have exterior friezes which tell a story you can join at any point, so that each viewer's sense of the story-sequence is different. And it is an essentially unstable vessel – you can rock it, or spin it. Quite a few dinoi have a whirligig on the bottom.

Like the other shapes which appear here, the cups vary in form and size to suit their particular usage; all of them appear as formal shapes in formal contexts, and all of them were also made without decoration for domestic use, even the *kantharos*, which is perhaps the least practical shape. Its high-swung handles would work better and be more durable in metal, and in fact that is how this shape probably originated. Some of the earliest metal examples of this kind of cup were made in bronze by Etruscan metalsmiths in northern Italy; there are later Etruscan examples, as there are of the kyathos ladle, made in a glossy dark grey or black ceramic imitating the metal version. The Athenians adopted the shape at the point when they were most deeply engaged with Etruria, and producing export versions of Etruscan pots with Athenian decoration for that market. The Athenian kantharos appears in vase-paintings as a special cup used by Herakles (Fig. 21) and Dionysos for formal parties; often it is used as a visual label to identify them. In reality, it is a delicate and unstable shape, and frequently does not survive intact. When it does, it is usually in an undisturbed tomb.

The *kylix*, to judge from its surviving numbers and representations of its use (Fig. 26), was the vessel of choice for symposia of all kinds. It varies considerably in size and width of bowl, and the versions of the shape which have high stems suggest that care was needed in use; drinkers are occasionally portrayed holding the cup in one hand by the stem, although the practical way to do so, at least with the largest ones, which can be nearly as wide as the drinker's body, is to support it with a hand under each handle. Spillage must have been common.

The *skyphos*, sometimes called a *kotyle*, was probably an equivalent of a beer mug, at least in capacity and potential for more practical and informal use. Like the kylix, it is often shown (see Fig. 26) as an item of party equipment, held in various ways. It survives in the plain black-glaze version for domestic use in large numbers, and was clearly a relatively convenient shape for the painter to decorate with a picture when required. The shape can be traced as far back as the eighth century BC at least; it looks like the cup of choice for virtually any occasion.

The *phiale*, in origin a shallow dish, often produced in metal, is represented on Athenian pottery most often as a ritual vessel for pouring libations to the gods. Black-glaze versions appear in domestic deposits, often with other vessels which support child care and other home-based activity – it presumably had many different uses, for both liquids and solids – food, baby wipes, and as an open container for small objects around the house.

## Uses and context: the symposium and its imagery

The kraters, cups, hydriai and oinochoai are all related to uses of wine and water, often together, and largely related to a social occasion familiar to all Greeks though in different formats: the symposium or formal drinking party. We are familiar with this term as the title of a famous dialogue by Plato, in which a philosophical discussion takes place during a party of this kind. The accounts we have, and the pictures which survive, tend to suggest an occasion designed to provide an inclusive atmosphere for a single-sex group, usually men, in which, at least in Athens, the participants were equals for the duration of the party. Each had a cup, each was served with wine from the central mixing bowl or krater, and all were encouraged by the atmosphere and the accessories for the party to think of themselves as belonging to an inclusive though democratic group.

Our major source of visual information about symposia is the illustrations on the black- and red-figure pottery of Athens, much of it designed to be used at such occasions, with a chronological concentration in the hundred years or so between the mid-sixth and the mid-fifth century – the century in which Athens got rid of its tyrants, repelled the Persians, and instituted a form of democracy, all things which were later recorded by the major historians of the period, and which were enshrined in some of the favourite mythological programmes used in classical temple sculpture. The way in which both the texts and the visual glosses deal with these events is to represent them as the achievement of the group of people who would, in peace time, be the participants in a symposium – the male citizens of military age, who as an army and a navy fighting as equals, had played a major part in establishing Greece in general and Athens in particular as a home fit for heroes, and a democratic one as well.

Much of our view of what the occasion was like depends on the pictures which appear on the pottery made for it. This constitutes much of the surviving output of the Athenian potters' quarter, the Kerameikos. Physically this was an area between the city centre, the Agora, and one of the main gates, outside which lay its major cemetery. It was a residential suburb, and part of it was the red-light district. The coincidence of function is a major factor in the very cohesive house style developed by pottery workshops of our period, and in its consensus of subject matter – their output was produced for a number of very well-defined purposes, and bought by a not very large group of people who would have understood its iconography, and appreciated what was done with it.

The subject matter itself could be said to fall into a few neat categories: mythological, genre pictures related to or actually illustrating everyday life, or crossover pieces in which the activity is everyday, but the personnel are mythological. The edges are blurred by the fact that deities, like heroes, are shown as human beings, and what they do is not actually very far removed from what humans do too. That, of course, is also the case in the Homeric poems, in which gods interfere with human activity, and also behave badly at parties.

Symposium pottery is often extremely self-referential: the reflexive principle can be seen at work on the many kraters which show symposia with heroic participants; the one shown in Fig. 25 (overleaf) is Corinthian rather than Attic, but there is no reason not to suppose that its function

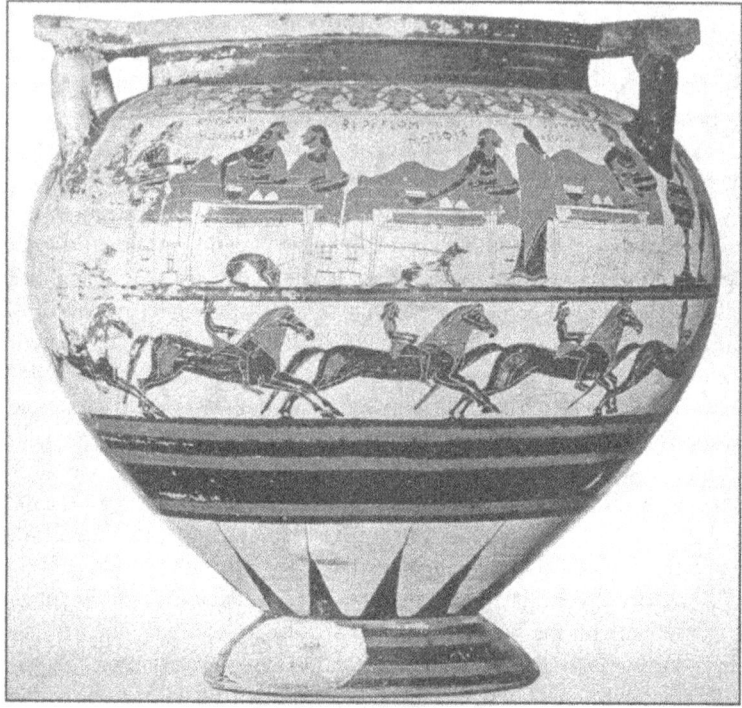

Fig. 25. Herakles with Eurytios. Corinthian krater. *c.* 600 BC. Louvre, Paris. H. 66 cm.

was the same. Herakles is the first Greek illustrated reclining at a symposium in the manner which later becomes standard for participants of whatever status. Here Herakles is a guest at a feast in the house of the king Eurytios, and his greedy eye has just lit on Eurytios' daughter Iole. Herakles is confidently propped on his elbow, holding his cup, and looking at the girl standing before him, watched by her father and brothers, evoking the tension caused by the appearance of Iole at the otherwise all-male feast and to foreshadow the tragic ending of the story in which Herakles demands the girl and kills his hosts and sacks their city when they refuse; this krater, like Odysseus' hospitality stories, is about the consequences of abusing the feast.

The symposium itself shows a string of klinai, or dining-couches, arranged around the vase with their drinkers, mirroring the reclining viewers of the krater in use. Below the feast is a band showing a horse-race. The association of the drinking party and an equine event on a big symposium vessel is not peculiar to Corinth. A number of Athenian volute kraters have double-decker strip-pictures on the neck which have the klinai and symposiasts, in an inside-out circle, and below them, a ring of chariots and horses. Those chariots and horses have a strong connotation with heroism, even Homeric heroism, and are there to suggest that the symposiasts, and the reclining viewers, are all at one with the heroic world, and the personnel have become continuous at least for the duration of the party. It is important to notice that the component parts of this set of images are very similar to those of the Geometric funeral images on the amphora Athens 804, discussed in Chapter 2, and the Hirschfeld krater, an equivalent grave-marker for a man, which has a Geometric chariot procession.

Some symposium crockery is self-referential in a more apparently documentary way: Fig. 26 shows a scene on a cup which presents us immediately with a vivid glimpse into a symposium in full swing. Here we can see the ambience very clearly – the partygoers are disposed round the cup in an arrangement which reflects that of the partygoers who will be looking at the cup, lying on their klinai in a circle. Some of the participants have brought their lyres (the ancient equivalent of a guitar) to the party, and at least one has been asked to play. He is singing as well. Another is playing kottabos – a game which must have been very messy, as it involved twirling your cup round your head and flicking the contents at a target; the target is not actually shown here, and probably the viewer of the cup at the symposium is to be read (and reads himself) as standing in for it. Certainly the cup itself is to be read, I think, as a picture of a very enclosed world, with an iconography and imagery of its own. In that

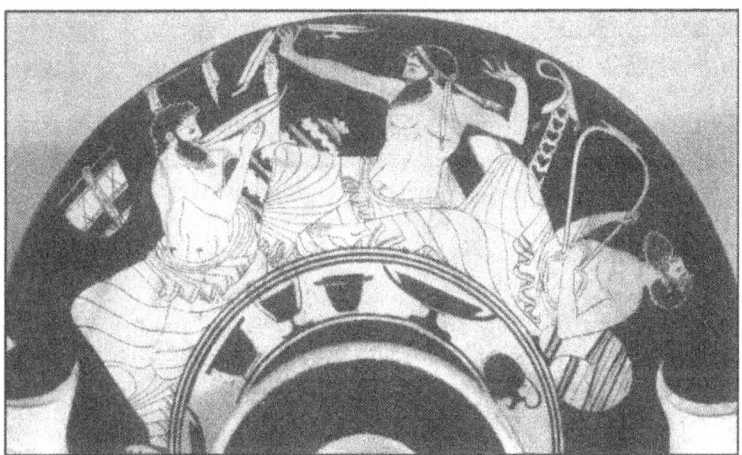

Fig. 26. Symposium. Attic red-figure cup painted by the Triptolemus Painter. c. 470 BC. Staatliche Museen. Berlin.

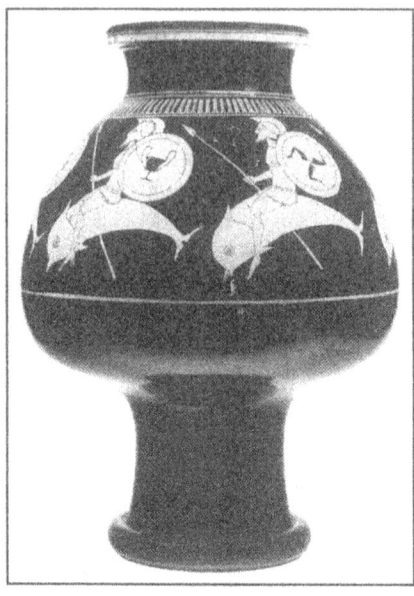

Fig 27. Dolphin riders. Attic red-figure psykter painted by Oltos, *c.* 500 BC. Metropolitan Museum of Art, New York, on loan from Norbert Schimmel Collection, King's Point. H. 30.2 cm.

world, the pictures on its utensils are there as a prompt, to keep the viewer in that milieu.

Quite a number of Greek wine vessels are designed to interact visually with the liquid they contain: the red-figure psykter, or cooler vase, in Fig. 27 is designed to contain ice or cold water, and float in the liquid it cools; the riders painted on it sing a song, which will be echoed by the symposiasts who view the pot, as they leap on their dolphins over the surface of that liquid, which should come up to the plimsoll line marked on the side. We also have evidence of another messy kottabos-like game which involved trying to sink objects floating on the wine in the central krater. The painter of our amphora, Exekias, also painted ships inside the rim of a large dinos, so that they would float on, and be reflected in, the wine within.

Much of our evidence suggests an occasion which was primarily designed as entertainment, though often with a serious social or political purpose. The Athenian symposium was at least partially intended to provide an inclusive glue to unite the men of military age, and their older and younger circle of friends and acquaintances, but had an educational purpose too; it is very easy to overlook the bonding process implied here as a way of providing a framework for the maturing male citizen in a context in which formal education was not used in that way. The symposium was obviously not training for the maturing citizen with an obligation to army or naval service, but one of its functions clearly was to situate him in a gathering of people whose assumptions about what was expected of them provided support and informal education as well as a group ethic. We have a more official parallel in the Spartan military mess or *syssitia* of the sixth and fifth centuries BC. This was, as all the evidence shows us, very much part of social inclusion and education via the so-called *agoge* or compulsory public upbringing for the Spartan male of citizen status. The expectation was that he would be part of the army for a long period, and education for that purpose, outside the home, began early. It is interesting to notice that the vast majority of figure-painted pottery produced in Sparta is of sixth-century date, and most of it is symposium related – largely cups, with some fine kraters; many of these are in black glaze, imitating the local bronzework, which is also among the finest which survives. Most of the known bronze kraters we have are of Spartan origin and workmanship. Comparatively little Spartan pottery of this period was exported; it seems to have stayed at home for specialised use in the symposium culture of the mess; its myth-pictures, as far as we can identify them, relate to local heroes and their cults, with a few examples of subject matter with currency all over Greece, such as the more memorable incidents of the Trojan War.

Most of our surviving decorated vessels, especially the unbroken ones, come from burial groups in a tomb, whether the burial was in Greece or in a colony, or in Italy, where Greek pots were traded as desirable merchandise with the Etruscans, and in the late fifth and fourth centuries made locally in the Hellenised cities of the south. The Greeks themselves, and the Italian cultures with whom they made contact, assumed an afterlife which was an enhanced version of the earthly one; the dead had therefore to be provided with the material goods they needed to take with them to Hades, and were buried with the major items of crockery which would support that afterlife. As a result, most surviving vessels come from burial sites; they may not have been produced specifically for burial, though some clearly were. They do, however, carry on the imagery and interests of those produced for the living into the tomb. The preoccupations with heroism, human or mythological, the social context to which the dead belong, some of the public images to which the family wanted to subscribe, are all catered for in the genre and myth scenes which appear on burial pottery, as they do on that intended for use in life. And the shapes which were produced for particular activities for the living reappear in the tomb. Occasionally we can make an educated guess that the funeral party made the final ceremony a form of symposium, with some cups made specially for this particular occasion, and left their vessels behind in the tomb; more often the collection is a little more random, and oil bottles and wine vessels appear together. And if the burial is cremation, the ash urn is often an amphora, occasionally with small vessels such as aryballoi inside, on top of the ashes of the dead.

Burial pottery is often gender-specific: female burials frequently have pottery with scenes which illustrate or parallel in myth the major ceremonials associated with birth, marriage and death, or domestic duty; some of the vessels themselves are specifically the ritual ones used for the ceremonies, or the domestic shapes decorated with images which have ritual connotations. Pyxides, for example, often show or refer to the chase and capture which was at least notionally part of the ritual of a wedding; an alabastron will often show the preparation of the bridal chamber for the bride. The pottery for a male burial will often relate in the same way to male use, and refer both to the activities of real life and to the myths which provide role models, exemplars and awful warnings.

# Chapter 4

# Scenes and Storytelling

Inevitably, we have already paid a little attention to the content of the pictures on Greek vases, but this chapter will discuss them in more detail; it is this, in some ways the most fascinating aspect of the study of Greek vases, and particularly Athenian ones, which interests the majority of scholars who use them to think about the culture of ancient Greece. Iconography is the name we give to this branch of pot-studies; iconographers concern themselves with content and techniques of visual communication. In this context this means that they study two major kinds of scene on Greek vases. First, they look at pictures of everyday life, and what they tell us about the Greeks that we would not otherwise know: i.e. how ancient Greece looked, and particularly how its inhabitants wanted to be seen, since we should not treat these pictures as documentary photography. Secondly, they look at scenes with a mythological content, with a particular interest in the way in which the Greeks told stories in pictures, how the stories change and ways of telling them, what they meant to their original viewers, and whether they have a meaning beyond the obvious.

The development of storytelling methods is fascinating in itself. More recently, scholars have begun to link the everyday life pictures with the mythological ones, and to see that some of them have important similarities of content and technique. In general, this sort of investigation is more fruitfully carried out with the detailed scenes on black- and red-figure vases of Athens of the sixth and fifth centuries BC, though they have earlier ancestors; this discussion will concentrate on the later vase scenes, though early ones will be mentioned where they shed light on their descendants.

As we saw in Chapter 3, the major occasions for the use of figure-decorated pottery were formal ones, such as religious rituals, and the symposium, or adaptations of its format to other ceremonies, and this had a profound effect on much of the subject-matter which appears. The other defining factor was a strong tradition of suiting the subject-matter, however obliquely, to the occasion of use, and the specialised purpose of the pot. We have seen, for example, how early funerary vessels began by showing the funeral itself and then incorporating imagery relating to status, wealth, and gender, and then mythological themes which would enhance these. The same process can be seen on vessels designed for other uses and groups of people. Eventually many vessels show scenes which relate more closely to everyday life; occasionally we have scenes of everyday life with mythological personnel, not unlike those which occur in ancient literature in which we discover heroines or goddesses weaving, or Odysseus building a boat.

## Everyday life and its images

If we think about everyday life broadly as a category which includes all the subject-matter which is definitely not myth, we find that we still have a very wide variety of material, some of it illustrating domestic activity, some of it dealing with civic or military occasions. Many of the domestic activities are related to traditional female work, many of those which take place outside are regarded as male ones; this is not, however, a hard and fast distinction, and there are some scenes which have very mixed messages and interpretations.

In particular, there has been a tendency to view scenes of female activity as reinforcing what we think we know about the lives they led, and the assumptions which underlay the way in which they were treated by the society within which they operated. Crudely, the assumption was that women, particularly those of citizen status, were expected to operate largely within the domestic circle, indeed largely within the house, with a very few official occasions on which they went out for ritual or sanctioned domestic purposes. It is beginning to be more widely recognised that this is a view influenced by texts which are often legal argument, or reporting and reacting to domestic court cases and legal decisions. These are very different from a descriptive account of how lives were actually led, and the impact of technical and legal status on everyday life may have been much less well defined than we used to think. Pericles' Funeral Speech, as presented by Thucydides (2.35-46), notoriously lays down the 'women should be little seen and never heard' view of the way in which proper women should behave; the evidence that this represents more than an idealist and legally-supported benchmark for Athenian or Greek society is patchy. There is quite as much evidence which suggests there was more variety and freedom for women than their legal position seems to have allowed. Some of the scenes of daily life which survive underpin that idea, and are now beginning to be looked at in their own right.

What is undeniable, though, is that there are a number of generic types of activity which associate women with the home and its needs in a

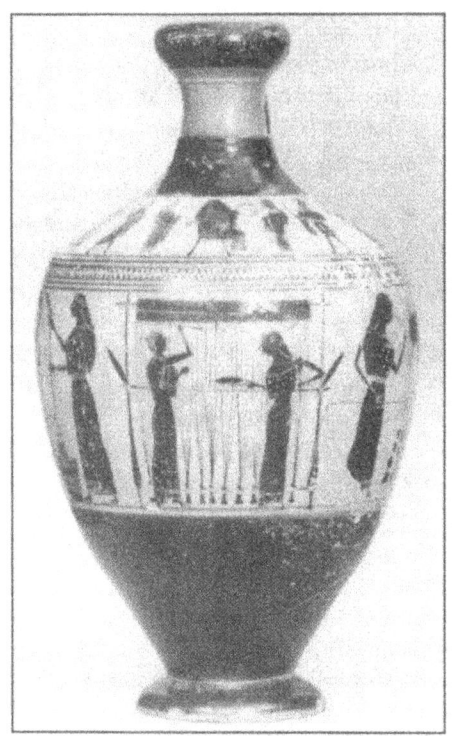

Fig. 28. Women weaving. Attic black-figure lekythos painted by the Amasis Painter, c. 540-530 BC. Metropolitan Museum of Art, New York. H. 17.2 cm.

pervasive imagery which is textual as well as visual. As soon as domestic images arrive on Greek vases, they show us women engaged in producing textiles (Fig. 28), looking after children, taking part in the domestically based rituals of marriage and funeral, fetching water – which may be one of the occasions of exit from the house, and occasionally taking part in public rituals, in some of which women had a substantial part to play. All of these activities are embedded in the imagery of the home in texts as early as the *Odyssey*, and remain fundamental to its presentation in poetry and drama as well as in the prose of everyday life.

The common scenes of domestic activity include textile production in all its stages, the world of the nursery, gardening; there is a group of late Athenian black-figure scenes of groups of women fetching water, which may have been produced to coincide with the building of a grand new fountain-house in Athens at that period; later red-figure shows single women fetching water from a more domestic well, perhaps to be viewed as being in the courtyard of the house. The Athenian red-figure of the latter part of the fifth century has more scenes which show group female activity, perhaps as reflection of the realities of a city at war, in which many of the men were away. It is in this context that we meet the scenes of women washing, group-bathing, dancing, and also reading and playing musical instruments, which undermine the conventional view of citizen women as an uneducated and largely imprisoned workforce. At the same point there is a visible upsurge in interest in scenes of children with toys, particularly miniature carts; a little earlier there was a vogue for scenes of boys in school, equipped with writing materials and musical instruments. There are even a few pictures of women holding a symposium; there is little consensus about their social status.

All these kinds of scene, and their extra-domestic equivalents, are studied not only for the nuances of interpretation they generate, but also for the much less controversial details of clothing, tools, furniture, and military equipment; there is no reason not to view these as effectively documentary records of the paraphernalia of everyday life which no one really bothered to describe contemporaneously, and as such valuable evidence. We can see changing fashions in clothing – essentially varying adaptations of the woven rectangle of cloth which can become the *peplos* or long sleeveless dress worn by women, the *chiton* which is its sleeved and pleated equivalent, and the male tunic and cloak worn at various lengths. The detail of a painting can show us the degrees of elaboration possible in the textiles used. Hairstyles, jewellery, footgear are all depicted in considerable detail. From vase paintings we can also see chairs, tables, storage furniture and containers, vessels in use, the loom and its accessory equipment. Much of this has perished in real life, so the illustrations of it are of great interest.

We have already seen that the symposium, or drinking party, and its surrounding activities is the most commonly portrayed male domestic event, though we should bear in mind that there were official versions of it which took place in other circumstances and in official premises rather than the host's house. It is usually presented as an all-male gathering at which wine was drunk, games were played, poetry and music were recited, serious political or philosophical discussion might take place, and it often finished with dancing to let off steam and counteract the after-effects of alcohol.

There are some representations which show larger gatherings with professional entertainers: often female musicians and dancers, and occasionally prostitutes. A number show sexual activity in this setting, both homosexual and heterosexual. Again, when we look at these pictures, we can incidentally learn about the sort of clothes these participants wore, if any, the crockery and musical instruments they used, the furniture and its textiles in the room, and even, perhaps, some of the people present. There are also a number of scenes showing men taking wine to the party, and the occasional visual comment on the drunken return home; this last is often in the bottom of a drinking cup, perhaps as a rather belated warning.

The dancing which can be part of the symposium can have a more organised and formal aspect, the so-called Komos, in which the dancers wear an exaggerated padded costume to perform a bottom-slapping, high-kicking dance. As time goes on, the dance remains in the domestic context without the costume (Fig. 22), and the costumed version mutates into a form of theatrical chorus. In this context, we begin to see other kinds of chorus in animal costume, and eventually satyrs, and then actors with other kinds of costume. Later paintings in red-figure show scenes which can be shown to be of theatrical productions, not of the mythological content of the plays. All of these pictures constitute valuable evidence for our knowledge of early theatre and of plays in performance. The volute krater shown in Fig. 13 may well, as we saw, show a scene from the *Eumenides* of Aeschylus in performance. The calyx krater from Southern Italy illustrated in Fig. 29 has a picture illustrating a phlyax play, a form of comedy which included burlesque.

Peacetime activity outside the house appears occasionally; probably it is limited by what it is physically easy to show, so that we see very little attempt to depict political activity, for example, but we do have a few scenes of olive picking, viticulture, ploughing and sowing, animal husbandry, food-sales, and trades such as shoemaking, carpentry or scent-marketing. Perhaps understandably, industries such as metalsmithing or

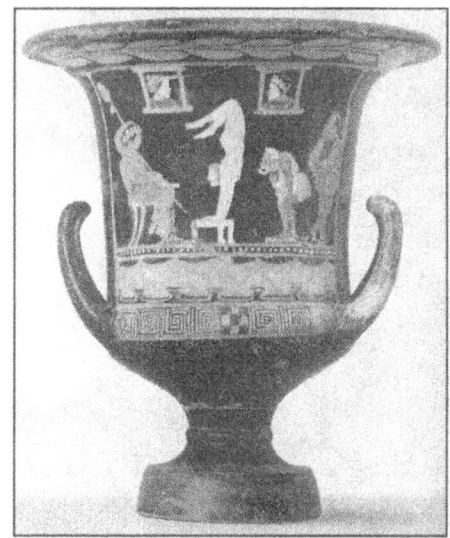

Fig. 29. Phlyax scene: female acrobat performing for Dionysos. Paestan red-figure calyx krater attributed to Asteas or more recently the Group of Louvre K 240. *c.* 350 BC. Museo Eoliano, Lipari. H. 39.3 cm.

the potter's shop are more popular. Equally understandably, much more attention is paid to high-status activity such as athletic competition, and religious ritual, which are easier to depict.

Images of religious rituals generally depict either the processional element, or a group of people engaged in the specifics of a sacrifice or a ceremony. Architectural settings, such as an indication of a temple, are rare, but a sacrifice scene will usually show the participants with the altar, occasionally carrying offerings in baskets or with the sacrificial animals. Very occasionally the recipient god, often Athena, is present. A few scenes, particularly in later red-figure, show women worshipping Dionysos, often represented as a mask hung on a pillar, with dance; a few others show men or women with a herm, the representation of Hermes, in his capacity as a fertility god, as a pillar with a bearded head and genitalia. Processions usually accompany a wedding or a funeral. They escort the bride to the groom's house, or arrive on the morning after with presents.

The archaic and classical Athenian funerary scenes are very closely related to their earlier counterparts: we see the laying out of the corpse, with the women in attendance (Fig. 30). Sometimes there will be a column or two to suggest the courtyard of the house in which this takes place. A procession accompanies the corpse on its way to the grave, female mourners tearing their hair and cheeks, males with a hand raised in

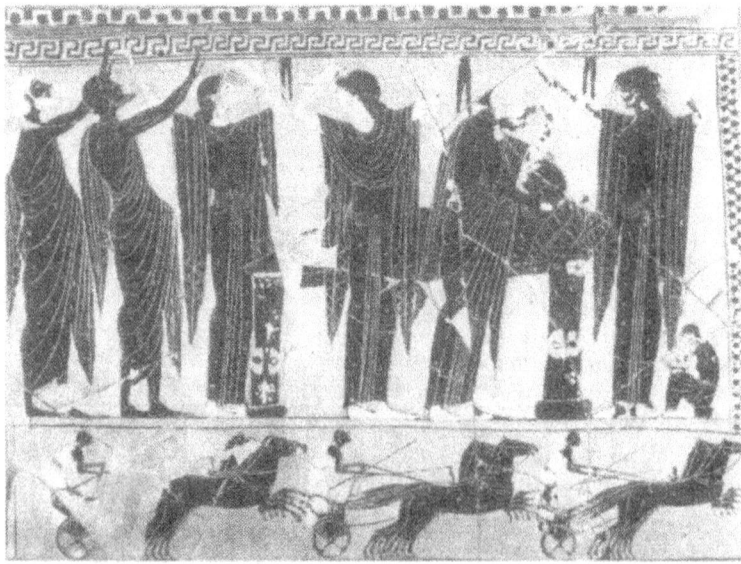

Fig. 30. Funeral. Detail of an Attic black-figure plaque. *c.* 510 BC. MM Auktion xiv, Basel.

farewell. Some sixth-century and many fifth-century burial vases show the tomb, often represented as a mound with a pillar, or just a pillar on steps, displaying offerings left behind by the living for the dead, and sometimes visitors tending the tomb.

Athletic activity is formalised on the Panathenaic prize vases, which show the event for which the vase was won: races on foot or on horseback, chariot races, boxing, and later, wrestling, discus, javelin, jumping, races in armour, and javelin throwing from horseback. All of these appear on other vessels in less formal contexts, together with scenes of the changing room and the fountain-house shower and massage. They gave the early red-figure painter, in particular, an opportunity to experiment with his approach to depicting the male nude. It would be fair to say that much male activity as shown on the vases is horse-related; the frontal chariot is a frequent subject, as is riding, leading or harnessing a horse. Occasionally the chariot is being driven as a part of a procession, often a wedding, occasionally as part of a funeral; some of the larger vase shapes lend themselves to processional scenes, and so provide a context in which these appear. Horses are raced, and occasionally part of a hunt, though this is more often a group male activity on foot.

Most male activity apart from the symposium is shown taking place away from the house. Departure from it for hunting, or more commonly for war, is a popular theme. Arming and departures are common in both black- and red-figure; the departing warrior is shown being handed the component parts of his kit, usually by his wife, as he puts it on. The later stages of the occasion involve a libation and possibly a farewell drink for the by now fully-armed warrior, perhaps in the presence of the wider family. In these pictures we see a changing panoply of armour and weapons; the major figure is usually a man wearing the standard breastplate or corselet, greaves, helmet, and sword. He will also have a shield and one or two spears. The hunting departure will show him in civilian dress with the spears and often a horse and a dog. The departure to war may, especially in late black-figure and early red-figure, show accompanying archers wearing striped knits and pointed caps, often thought to reflect real Scythian archers from the Black Sea area, introduced to Athens by the tyrant Peisistratos as a specialist police force.

Fighting is one of the earliest subjects to appear on figured Greek vases; we might view it as a logical development of the militarily related imagery of the early funerary vessels. The early fights are in some ways more ambitious – the occasional naval battle or shipwreck appears on Geometric vases more than on later ones. The later ones more often show hand-to-hand fighting by pairs of warriors, which can be multiplied to form a battle scene on a larger vessel – much the same principle as that used by the Homeric epics to describe a battle via a composite made up of single combats. The fights can be between horsemen, or infantry, or combinations of both; they can have watchers, or auxiliary fighters. And we also see the aftermath, as a body is fought over or carried off the field. As with the domestic scenes, the details of armour and equipment are presented realistically, and subject to changes of fashion over time.

**Myth and narrative strategies, experiments, and mistakes.**

The study of myth and narrative on vases is both interesting in itself and intrinsically related to the study of representations of real-life. Broadly, the myths depicted relate to the large cycles of stories about the Trojan War and its aftermath; Herakles, which involves more than the twelve labours which became canonical in the fifth century; Theseus and other major heroes such as Perseus, especially with Gorgons; the gods collectively, especially their fight with the giants; specific incidents in some of the more popular gods' careers, or representing their individual functions, such as Apollo's prophetic activities; generic scenes involving Dionysos; monsters, or representatives of otherness, such as centaurs or Amazons. Many of these develop standardised formats or personnel in the pictures which represent them: we can expect, for example, to find a black-figure Herakles fighting the lion watched by Athena and his nephew Iolaos. Dionysos will usually be accompanied by satyrs and maenads. In the same way there are some frequently repeated incidents of the Trojan War, which are easy to recognise from the way in which they are arranged, and from the actions, dress and possessions or attributes of the people involved.

In Chapter 2 we looked at a Geometric picture of a funeral on Athens 804, and it was implied that that sort of scene was the beginning of narrative art. Although it is in itself a static picture, and its style is restrictive, it shows figures engaged in an immediately recognisable activity, made so by their gestures and the presence of the body on its bier. One of the most basic principles of narrative art is that the viewer should be able to identify the people portrayed, and through them, the action or story in which they are involved. There are some Geometric vases which try to tell stories, not altogether successfully, but show this principle beginning to evolve.

One very interesting example appears on a four-legged stand from the Kerameikos cemetery in Athens. On one leg (Fig. 31) is a figure of a hulking man fighting off a ferocious quadruped with some sort of trian-gular-bladed weapon. It is easy to read this as Herakles and the Lion. We

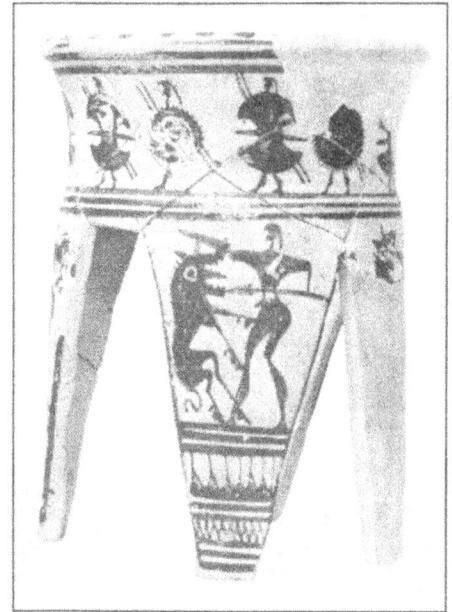

Fig. 31. Lion fighter. Attic
Geometric tetrapod stand,
eighth century BC.
Kerameikos Museum.
Athens. H. 17.8 cm.

can argue that this is an early version of the story, in which the idea that the lion is invulnerable to cutting weapons is as yet not a feature; and it is clear that the artist had never seen a lion, although he knew that it had four legs, claws and teeth. Matters become more complicated, though, if we look at another leg of the stand, and see that there the man could be viewed as wearing a skin; do we now read this as an early version of the kind of Herakles and the Lion picture in which he wears the skin while fighting the lion from which he got it? Or do we say that the whole thing pre-dates Herakles as subject matter, and this is an imitation of a Near Eastern motif, seen on furniture mounts and decorative metalwork, which will later be explained for the viewer by the invention of the story of Herakles in the Greek world? What did the artist intend us to understand by this? Is it mythological at all? We tend to assume it is because by the time this was painted, lions were not native to Greece, and there is a long Near Eastern tradition of depicting kings and heroes fighting or hunting lions, which we can argue translated itself to Greece along with the artefacts on which such representations occur.

In Chapter 2 we looked at the Berlin Painter's image of Herakles with the tripod (Fig. 14). We know that he is Herakles because he carries a club and wears a lion skin. In this at least we are on an equal basis with an Athenian viewer seeing this for the first time in about 500 BC. That viewer

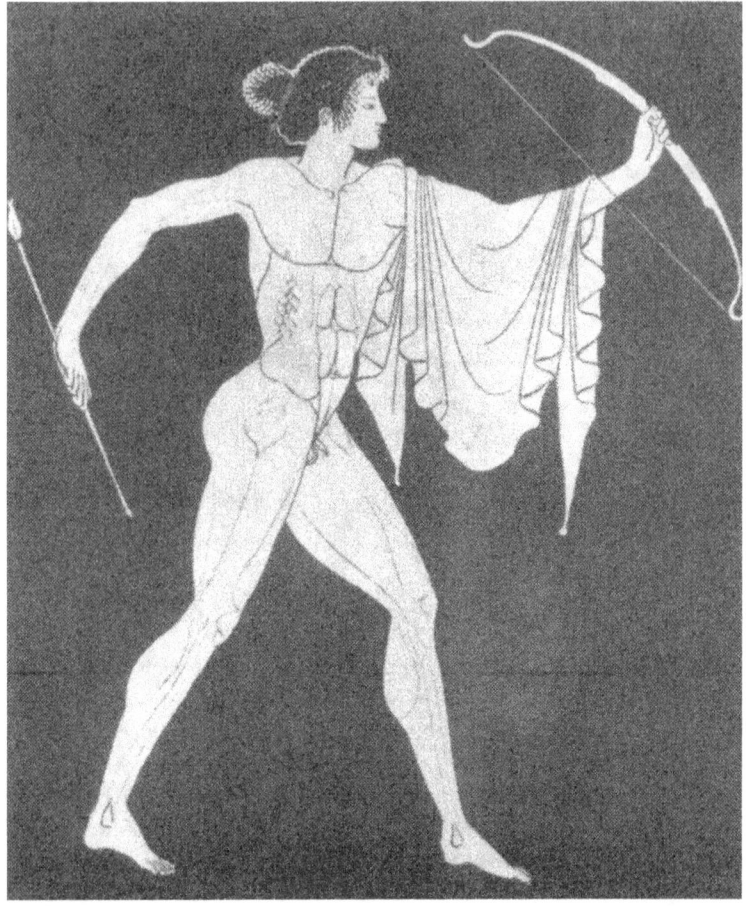

Fig. 32. Apollo. Detail of an Attic red-figure amphora painted by the Berlin Painter. *c.* 500 BC. Martin von Wagner Museum. Würzburg

would be likely to know about the circumstances in which the club and more particularly the lion skin were acquired.

Herakles is carrying another object over his shoulder: a tripod cauldron. This should lead the viewer into asking why he should be carrying such an object, and one natural, and partly subconscious, process here is to dredge up an episode of Herakles' career involving one. The obvious answer is the story of his trip to Delphi and his theft of the tripod of Apollo, with the subsequent battle over its recovery.

In fact this vase is two-sided, and on the other side (Fig. 32) is Apollo. If we look at Herakles, we see that he is looking over his shoulder in a way which implies pursuit, and Apollo's posture also suggests that he is chasing something, so whichever side of the pot you see first, you are led to look at the other. This is quite a common way of using the pot itself, incidentally, to imply movement, and so to tell a chase story. Now, with the advantages of hindsight, we know that there is a visual tradition of a generic fight over a tripod from the seventh century BC. Here neither participant is identified by anything inherent in the picture. The earliest representations in which they are belong to the mid-sixth century, and from then on they are quite popular. The implied chase appears almost immediately the personnel are identified, and extras soon appear too, including Zeus, who appears to have been brought in to intervene when the going got rough. What we do not have is a contemporary verbal version. The later writers Diodorus and Apollodorus tell us a story which would account for the pictures; Pausanias gives a version of the story in an account of a statue group at Delphi (10.13), and says that the poets took up the story; if they did, we have no knowledge of it. What we do have feeds into this discussion, though, in a number of ways.

One important aspect of attempts to explain the nature of narrative art turns on whether narrative is synonymous with illustration or not. It has often been assumed by the text-based scholar that mythological pictures are illustrations of textual material which no longer exists, but once did. This position is now changing because we recognise that it assumes general literacy in the Greece of its period, and an established text base, which we now recognise was non-existent, and it does not allow for variants or originality or experiment by the individual painter or sculptor, all of which can be shown to exist. Nowadays the classical art historian would argue instead for an oral story, in itself capable of infinite variation and embellishment, which may lie behind such pictures as a general notion, but not that they are an illustration of an accepted published story, an ur-text, in any form. What a picture such as this does assume, and a number of scholars have now written about this aspect, is prior knowledge of the story; we have to know about Herakles' visit to Delphi before we can explain the individual features of this and other similar pictures – he is not carrying an expensive cooking pot for nothing: it means something.

The inclusion of meaningful objects is, of course, a feature of narrative art of all kinds; and they may have more than one role, or fit into more than one category. The use of attributes – objects which the figure wears or carries as an identifier, or as part of a system of identifiers – is essential to narrative art of this sort, especially in the absence of textual accompaniment. Herakles' lion skin is a badge which tells us who this beefy

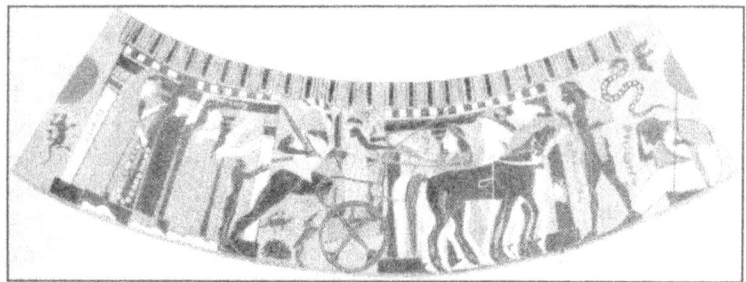

Fig. 33. Departure of Amphiaraos. Detail of Corinthian krater painted by the Amphiaraos Painter. *c.* 580 BC. Now lost, once Staatliche Museen, Berlin.

individual is; in fact it has a bigger frame of reference than that – it reminds the viewer about the circumstances of its acquisition, the twelve Labours, and so on. It is also protective, because the skin was invulnerable to cutting weapons, and so it is balanced by the cloak over Apollo's corresponding arm. Apollo's bow and arrows work in the same way as Herakles' skin – a label with resonances.

Another example will lead into a slightly different angle on the use of the familiar. Fig. 33 shows the shoulder scene from a Corinthian krater of the early sixth century, which depicts a very rare scene from the Theban cycle – the departure of the Seer Amphiaraos. He knows that if he goes to take part in the conflict over the Theban succession, he will not return. He has, however, been stitched up by the gods and his wife, who has been given a necklace as a bribe to make him go.

Now the departure scene is a commonplace in Greek art, as it was, no doubt, in life. It has several standard forms, but most of them involve the warrior and his wife or parents or both, who may hand him parts of his armour, or pour a libation in the hope of his safe return. A cavalry version will involve a chariot or a horse. This is often a generic scene from everyday life, but it is also one which can be adapted for use as an illustration, or visual version of, a specific mythological occasion – Hector arming, or Achilles' new armour. Topographical and architectural settings are rare; the position of the female figure in a supporting role, often as a framing figure drawing attention to the warrior, is standard.

The Amphiaraos vase works by using a familiar format – the vehicular departure scene – and differentiates it from any old standard departure by the architectural setting and the placement of Eriphyle as the almost excluded figure at the very edge of the group of household supporters, holding the significant object which is the key to the whole story. And

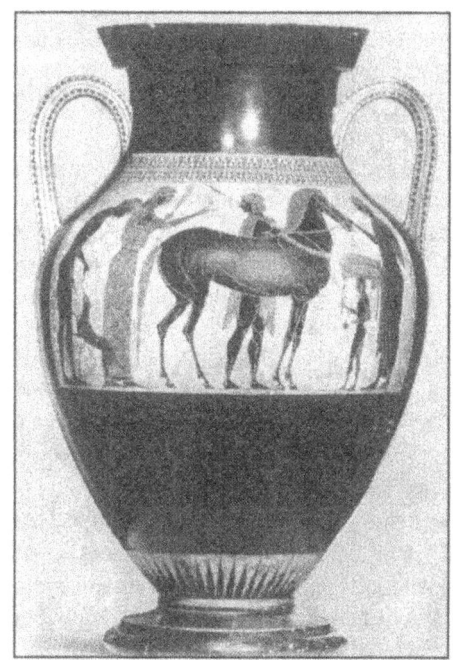

Fig. 34. Kastor and
Polydeukes – homecoming
or departure? Attic
black-figure amphora painted
by Exekias, c. 540-530 BC.
Vatican Museums, Rome.
H. 61 cm.

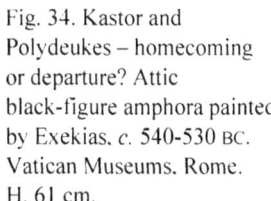

Amphiaraos, still in the home from which he knows he is departing never to return, looks back at her – an ambivalent look in this context.

The other side of the Ajax and Achilles amphora (Fig. 34) also shows, as we saw in Chapter 2, a scene related to and using the departure scene as its format. This involves the Dioskouroi, Kastor and Polydeukes, their mother and stepfather Leda and Tyndareus, the dog, the horse, and a boy carrying an aryballos and a stool with clothing folded on its seat. The major characters and the horse are labelled, so that we have to include their identity into our reading of the scene. The scene is a subtle and complicated one, but it would be possible to argue that it uses the home-imagery of everyday life scenes to inform this mythological one; the dog, the horse, and the spears can be associated with a departure for the hunt, more perhaps than one for war. The aryballos and the garment on the stool suggest a bath, and therefore a return rather than a departure. Parents and sons, the nuzzling dog, and Tyndareus' pat on the nose for the horse, together with the textiles of Leda's dress and Castor's red cloak, and the flower Leda holds out, are all powerful images of the home and domestic activity. And there may also be a link with the other side of the vase, on which Ajax and Achilles, detached from home and everyday reality, wearing cloaks made at home for them, and the armour which symbolises their departure from it, focus on an activity which will shut out the war. This side of the vessel probably originated a striking icon, the other uses a well-worn version of a real life event to create an ambivalent picture of heroism.

It would be wrong to pretend that there are no Greek pictures which illustrate an identifiable text. By the time the picture (Fig. 35) of the Ransoming of Hector, in book 24 of the *Iliad*, was painted by the Brygos Painter, we can be fairly sure that there was a standardised version of the epic in existence. What is interesting here is what the artist had to do to make sure that his viewers recognise the scene for what it is. You see that Achilles is lying on a kline or couch beside a food-table, looking towards the boy who is fetching him a drink. Priam approaches from the left, accompanied by a posse of people carrying objects. Under the kline is the body of Hector, conspicuously bleeding. If we look at the text of *Iliad* 24 itself we will find that Achilles has just finished eating, and the table is still beside him, as are two companions who are not shown in this illustration, but who appear on the original vase. Priam, however, is alone, and has left the ransom in the cart in which he came. We are not told about the whereabouts of Hector's body during this encounter with Achilles, but the likelihood of its being under Achilles' kline is small, and we are told that any damage it sustained while being dragged round the walls of Troy behind Achilles' chariot was repaired immediately by the gods.

What has evidently happened here is that the artist has solved his identification problem by showing us a number of the salient features of the story at once; some critics would probably argue that this is an example of what is sometimes called synoptic storytelling – a picture which combines features of a story which are chronologically sequential in its

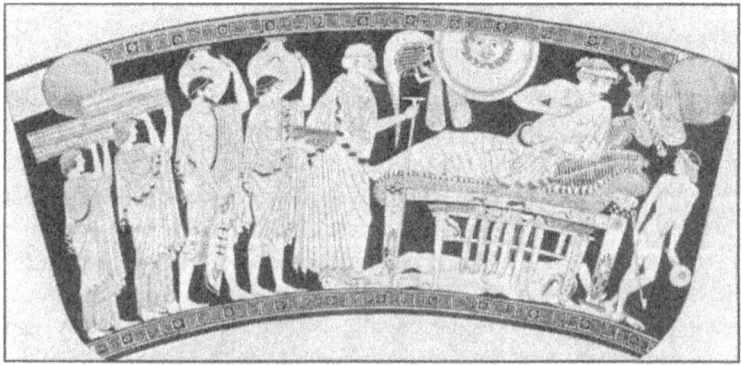

Fig. 35. Ransoming of Hector. Detail of Attic red-figure skyphos painted by the Brygos Painter. *c.* 500 BC. Kunsthistorisches Museum. Vienna.

textual version, in a single image. We could argue, however, that it is more a question of making sure that the viewer has a pointer to the most important bits of the tale, and that it activates some of his social assumptions. The depiction of Achilles as if he were a symposiast, reclining at one of those Athenian drinking parties which were so much else as well, is meant to resonate for the viewer too; heroic myth appears on symposium crockery to incorporate the drinker into the heroic world while he uses it, and this representation makes Achilles one of the boys. We could say the same about the image of Herakles (Fig. 21) discussed in Chapter 2: there is no story, as such, to this. Here he is in Olympus being feasted by Athena on his arrival after he had retired and become a god himself. Here the victory feast and also the funeral feast are part of the frame of reference; the kline, which is also a bed, and a bier, as well as an important part of the symposium furniture, is an active reminder of this network of associations. Feasting is the thing that humans, heroes and gods have in common; sometimes they do it together, and wine is the agent of association, the afterlife, and apotheosis.

We can also say that this image relates to a rather later trend in Athenian vase painting, in which a god or hero is shown by themselves, without a narrative context, but often with attributes which suggest one, or which suggest a characterisation or personality for them. Our image of Ajax and Achilles playing a board game can be seen as another early example of that kind of image. Here there is an extra factor, in the shape of inscriptions; Ajax and Achilles are labelled, because otherwise neither we nor the ancient viewer would have been able to identify them. The scene seems to have originated with Exekias, the author of this version of it, and generated a number of later examples and adaptations. So there was nothing but his inscriptions to go on, and there is no corresponding myth or tradition which it illustrates. The figures also have speech balloons which seem to refer to the score: Ajax has thrown three, and Achilles four. Achilles is the dominant figure, retaining his helmet, Ajax is the loser, and the speech inscriptions are there to tell us so. I argue that the other two images of Ajax, not at this stage a popular hero, in Exekias' surviving repertoire, also support the idea of him which we find in Homer and later, as a great hero who is also a loser – someone who commands enormous respect, but comes off second best. Another shows him carrying the body of his friend Achilles off the battlefield, and yet another (Fig. 36) his later suicide, after he has lost Achilles' armour to Odysseus in a competition.

All of this depends, though, on the labels, and it is possible to interpret the picture quite differently. The board game, and the partying Herakles, belong to a select group of images which are either new versions of old

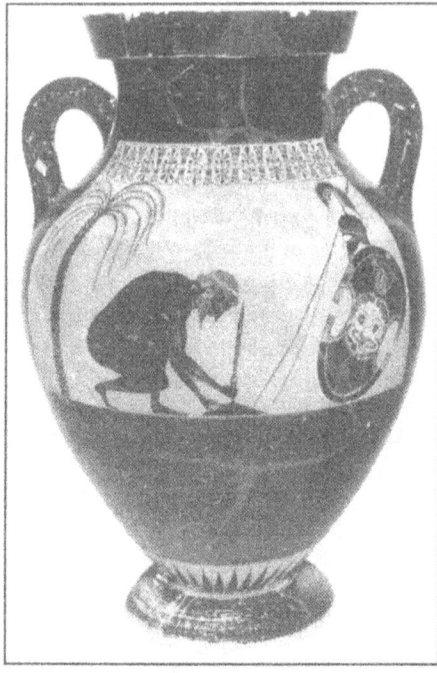

Fig. 36. Ajax's suicide.
Detail of an Attic black-
figure amphora by Exekias.
540-530 BC. Boulogne
Museum. H. 54 cm.

stories, or completely new images or situations involving known characters, which belong to the latter half of the sixth century in Athens, and are
therefore chronologically connected with the reign of the tyrant Peisistratos. Their emergence and equally abrupt disappearance over about
thirty years at that point has led one influential group of scholars to argue
very ingeniously for a direct connection between these images and the
politics of the time – Herakles represents Peisistratos, and from that
position it is possible to make very close connections between some of
the images concerned and specific events: in other words to argue that
these images are effectively political or social cartoons. In this context the
stories in Herodotus about Peisistratos effecting a coup d'état by dressing
up a tall girl as Athena and getting her to drive him to the Acropolis
(*Histories* 1.60), and taking a defending Athenian army by surprise
because they had settled down after a picnic to play dice (1.63) lead to a
view of our two pictures and their subtext which is quite different from
the previous one, though it still depends on identification of the figures,
however it is done.

   The need for prior knowledge of the story, and the assumption that
identification of the figures is necessary are well worn academic positions;
but if we tend towards believing that we need the knowledge and the

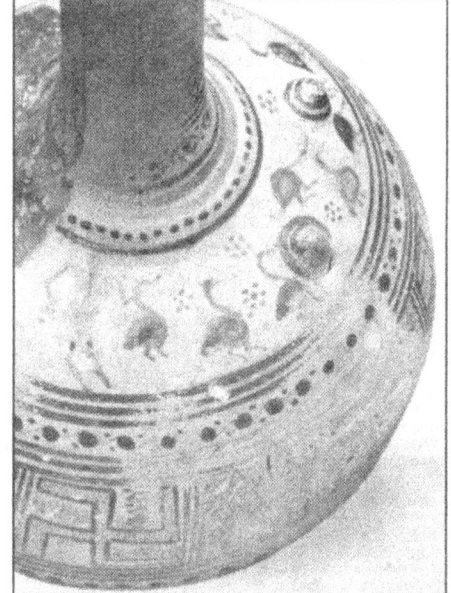

Fig. 37. Detail of an Attic Geometric jug. *c.* 750 BC. Ny Carlsberg Glyptothek. Copenhagen.

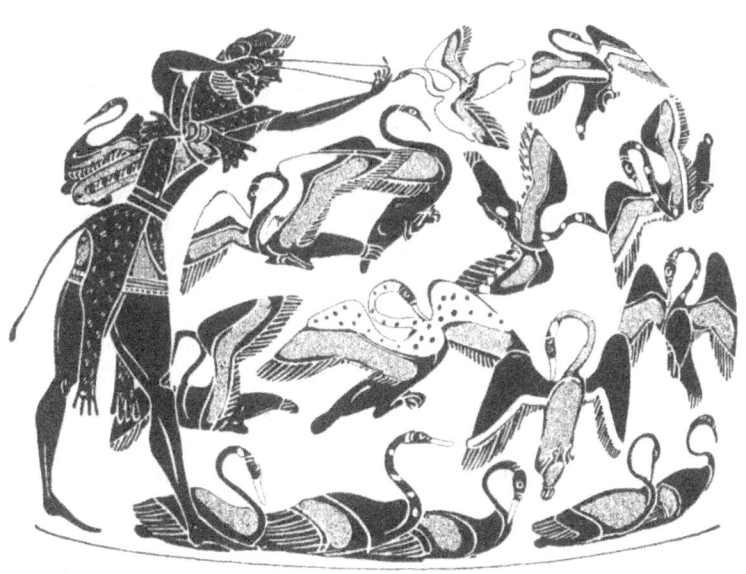

Fig. 38. Herakles and the Stymphalian birds. Detail of an Attic black-figure amphora. Group E. *c.* 545 BC. British Museum. London.

identifiers, we can look at failures of communication and experiments as profitably as the successes. A Geometric vase now in Copenhagen shows (Fig. 37) a man holding a bird by the neck; in front of him run other birds around the shoulder of the jug. The great temptation is to identify this as the earliest picture we have of Herakles and the Stymphalian birds; Fig. 38 shows what it looks like two hundred years later, where we can be sure – Herakles has a catapult, and wears his lion skin. In the absence of any such indicators, our Geometric man could just as well be a distressed Attic poultry farmer.

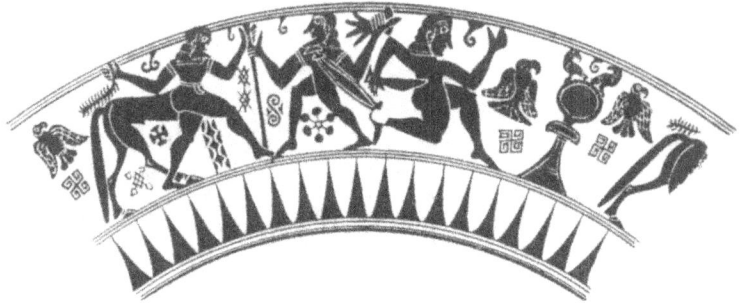

Fig. 39. Drawing of detail from a Protocorinthian aryballos painted by the Ajax Painter. Museum of Fine Art, Boston.

Centaurs provide another example of the effects of expectation and insufficient knowledge: the horse/man hybrid is a shape which we immediately identify as a centaur, but we should be very clear that that is because this particular monster turns up in narrative contexts in which we know that the monster involved *is* a centaur. In fact we can argue that the concept takes time to evolve; an early seventh-century painting (Fig. 39) showing a fight between a thunderbolt-wielding humanoid and a horseman hybrid has no readily recognisable context. Thunderbolts are associated with Zeus, but if that applies here, then we lack an encounter with a centaur. What if the monster in this scene is actually something else? A giant, for example? If so, then we do have a battle which this could illustrate.

Then there is a delightful scene from a relief pithos from Boiotia (Fig. 40) which shows an unmistakable Perseus decapitating Medusa, shopping-bag under his armpit awaiting the head. We are familiar with Medusa as an essentially leonine creature, at least facially, with a human body. This one is a horse-woman hybrid, and the woman is wearing a skirt, at the back of which the horse body emerges. The effect is absurd rather than frightening, and makes it quite obvious why that particular vision of

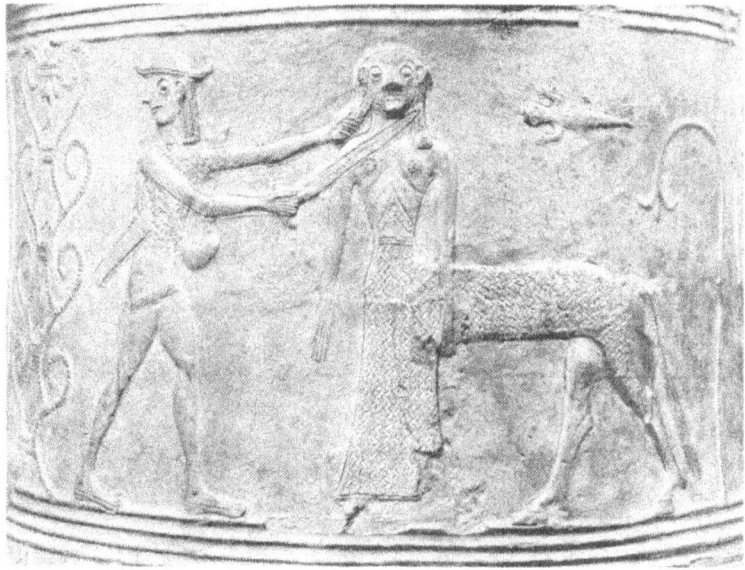

Fig. 40. Perseus and Medusa. Detail of relief amphora from Boiotia, early seventh century BC. Louvre, Paris.

Medusa, and for that matter centaurs, never gained popularity – centaurs do not wear skirts with conviction.

If we start from the idea of a gradually-evolving standard version of a story recognisable to everyone, then we can play with the idea of nuanced excerpts from it. The Perseus story is a good example. A dinos by the Gorgon Painter (Fig. 41, overleaf), is one of the earliest versions of it, dating from the first twenty years of the sixth century. The single mythological scene is at the top, and below it are bands with animals and monsters, or florals.

The scene, which gives the painter his conventional name, is a version of the Perseus and Medusa story which gives us the whole chase, Medusa collapsing, her sisters pursuing Perseus, our hero himself, his divine supporters, and his getaway chariot, which forms the punctuation which the painter evidently felt that he needed – it is one of a pair framing a fight which is both the end and the beginning of the Perseus frieze, otherwise a continuous strip around a vase which has no handles to break it up.

By the mid-century, when the dinos has become much less popular, the Amasis Painter, and others, are treating the scene as a metope containing a three-figure composition as metopes do: in this case (Fig. 42)

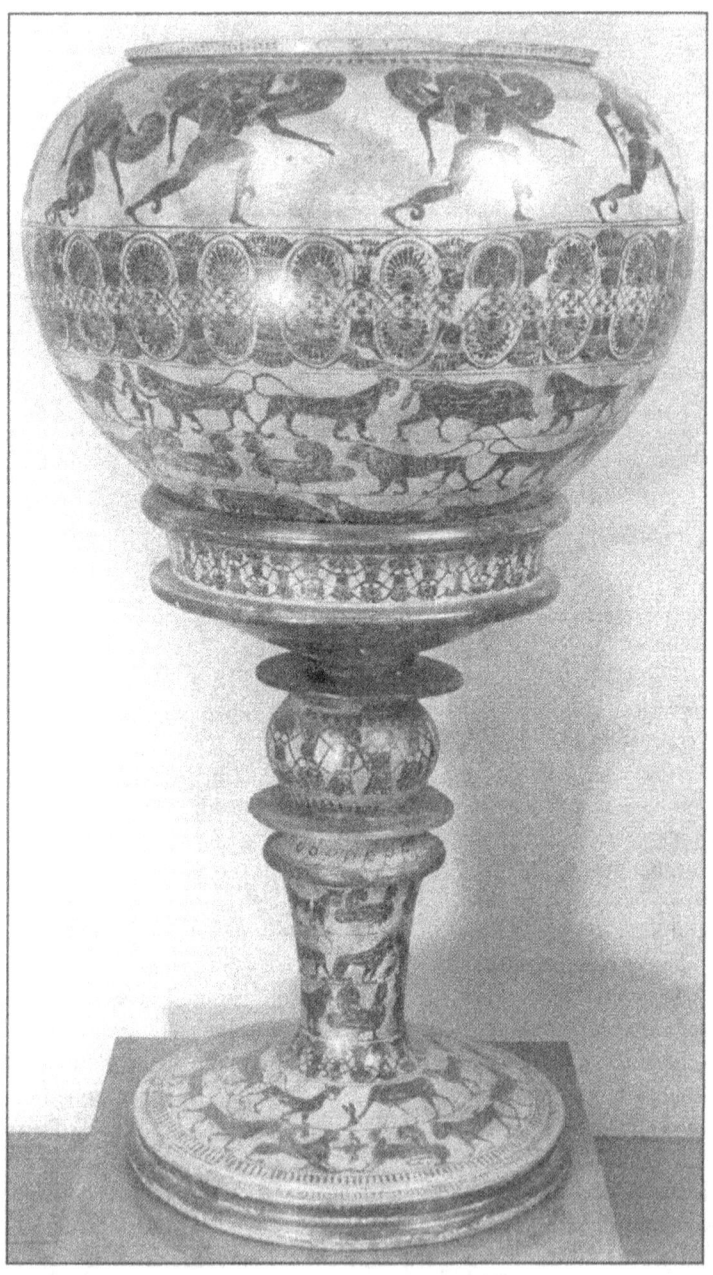

Fig. 41. Attic black-figure dinos and stand painted by the Gorgon Painter. *c.* 500
BC. Louvre, Paris. H. 93 cm.

Fig 42. Perseus and Medusa. Attic black-figure olpe painted by the Amasis Painter. c. 540 BC. British Museum, London. H. 26 cm.

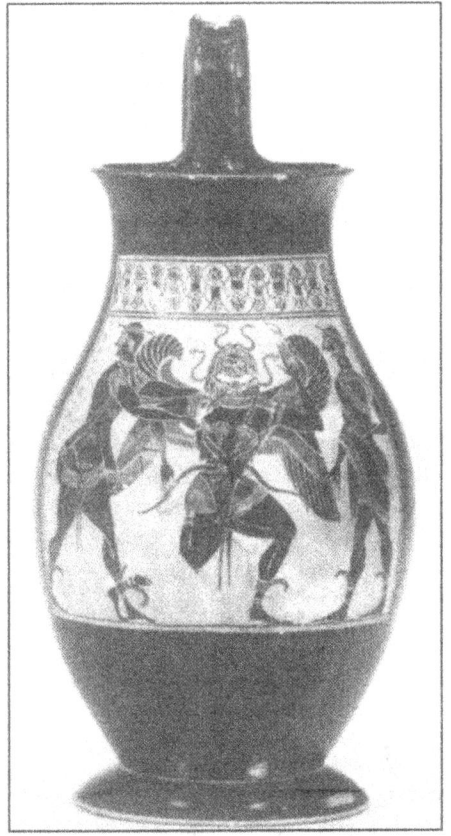

Medusa, still possessed of her head, in the centre, and Perseus and Hermes as framing figures. It is this composition, with variable personnel, which persists, and not the processional version, which is there to fill a continuous frieze.

The Gorgon Painter has the decapitated Medusa, her pursuing sisters, the fleeing Perseus, and two bystanders, one of whom is Hermes, and the other may be Athene. Metope versions tend to have Medusa, Perseus, and one of the two gods, though there is a Corinthian painted metope from Thermon which has Perseus with the head in a shopping bag, and there is a pediment from Corfu with Medusa and her two children, but no Perseus. Notice, though, that where the presentational format demands a small number of figures, a choice has been made about which figures to use, and therefore what to imply or emphasise about the story. The Corinthian metope is about the success of the expedition; the versions which show a divine helper are reminding us (via the choice of helper illustrated) about the instructions given Perseus by his various sources of help as well as about the fact that he had it. The pursuing sisters cease to be important very quickly, and eventually we have a non-monstrous Medusa, though Perseus still has to look away from her.

This sort of nuanced excerpting of a story is not rare: we could look at the François Vase (Fig. 9), a huge krater now in Florence, found in fragments in Etruria, recovered over several digging seasons around 1845, and smashed and mended several times since. One of its many friezes (Fig. 43) shows a popular episode from the Trojan War. Troilos, one of King Priam's sons, went with his sister Polyxena to water his horses at a fountain outside the walls of Troy. They were ambushed by Achilles, and Troilos was killed; Polyxena escaped temporarily, leaving her broken water-pot behind her. In this picture, we have the fountain house, labelled 'fountain' in case we do not recognise what it is, and beside it Achilles' divine fan club. Then comes Achilles, Troilos on horseback, his sister's hydria, and the girl herself running away, watched by her father and his old counsellor Antenor.

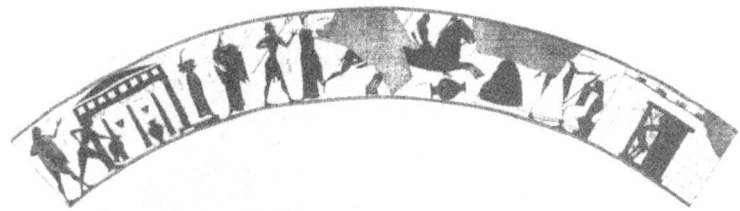

Fig. 43. Detail of the François Vase. Athenian black-figure volute krater by Kleitias and Ergotimos. c. 570 BC. Museo Archeologico. Florence.

Now there are other pictures of this story, and from them we discover that there is no need to use labels, and there is little evidence that literacy was at all general among pot-painters or their clients. Secondly, we discover that elements of the story can be left out, so that there are versions without Achilles, showing the dropped and broken water jar, and Polyxena and Troilos making off, or either of the runners can be omitted, we do not need the fountainhouse or the spectators, and sometimes we just have Achilles lying in wait. All these are, as it were, excerpts from a notional full version, and from them we can see that the whole version was so thoroughly understood that it was possible to refer to the whole story without showing all of it.

So far we have not looked at emotional content or relationships as a part of narrative. Not all narrative art tries to express or use emotion,

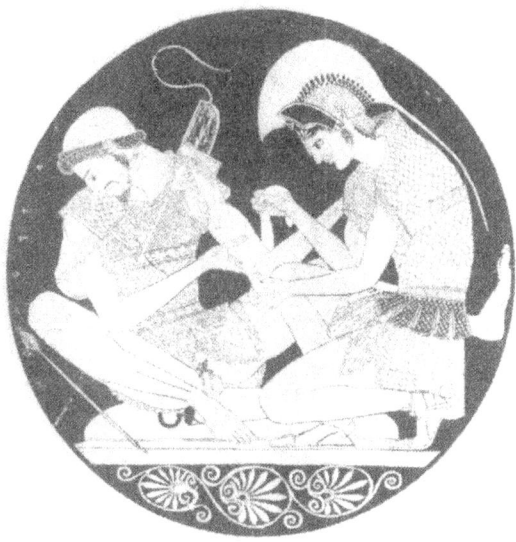

Fig. 44. Achilles bandages Patroklos. Detail of an Attic red-figure cup painted by the Sosias Painter. *c.* 510-500 BC. Staatliche Museen. Berlin.

though most narrative needs to involve more than one person, and therefore an expressed or implied relationship, even if it is simply an action of a superficial kind. If it involves a single frame, then the artist is going to have to muster quite a lot of tools to express anything beyond the one figure doing something to or with another. Faces are traditionally seen as having little to do with the way in which Greek art works, largely because faces in this context are very stylised, and there seem to have been other ways of saying the same things. But there is always the exception which does point to an interest in the inner life, or a developing relationship. The cup tondo by the Sosias Painter shown in Fig. 44 does use both body language and facial expressions, including the white paint to enhance Patroklos' clenched teeth, to show us a tense and painful moment. Exekias' picture of Ajax's suicide (Fig. 36) is a striking attempt in a very unpromising medium, using all the narrative tools at its disposal, but with much of the restraint of Greek tragedy, to involve us in the hero's despair.

So every picture can tell a story; not all narrative art has to involve identifiable people, nor must it involve a known myth. Conversely, not all scenes showing identifiable heroes are narrative, and we lose a lot if we are too prescriptive about how we read these scenes, or about the methodologies we employ for doing so, or if we expect there to be one right way of doing it. We will gain more if we can allow for experiments,

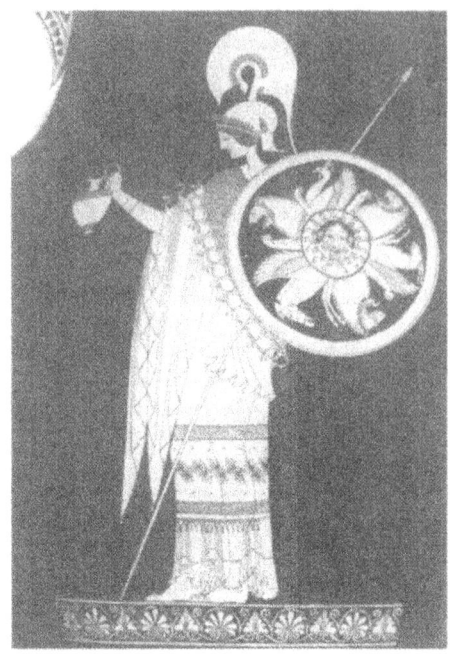

Fig. 45. Athena. Attic
red-figure amphora painted
by the Berlin Painter. *c.* 500
BC. Antikenmuseum. Basel.
H. 79 cm.

mistakes, Friday jobs along with the undeniable successes, and probably much nearer the truth about how the features we now take for granted evolved.

Two further things we should emphasise are that many of the myth scenes appear on pottery intended for the symposium, which may be re-used as funeral crockery, and that some stories or people are more popular than others. If we see a picture of Athene (Fig. 45) in full armour, it may mean no more than its apparent face value; but if we realise that she is carrying the same shield and spear as every Athenian male bore when he went into battle as part of the army, then this image immediately means much more, and her appearance on a wine jar for a symposium can be explained as a picture designed to support the drinker's self-image. Why is she holding a jug? If we turn the pot, we see that on the other side (Fig. 46) is Herakles. He, too, is a favourite hero, because after an eventful career he eventually succeeded in conquering death and going to heaven, where, on this pot, his patron goddess and helper is pouring him a much-needed drink.

This kind of association of themselves with the myth by the original viewers is one of major reasons for the continued production of figured pots like this in Athens, and it is interesting to notice, whatever the

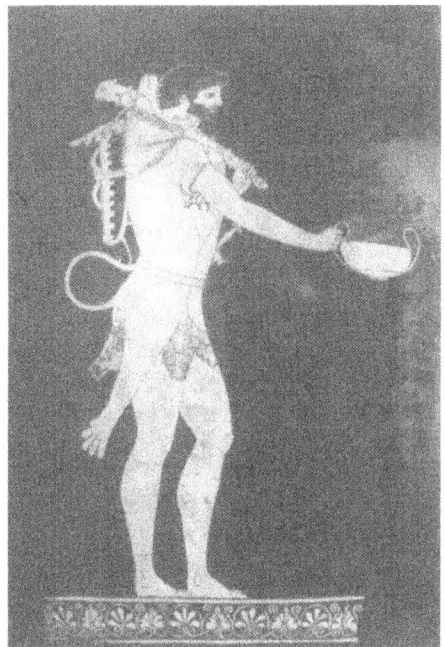

Fig. 46. Herakles. Detail of
Attic red-figure amphora
painted by the Berlin Painter.
c. 500 BC. Antikenmuseum,
Basel.

implications of the observation, that as we saw earlier, the myths become
less common, and the pictures of everyday life, especially those involving
women, become commoner in the later fifth and fourth centuries, when
the Athenians are involved in the Peloponnesian War and the men are
fighting, and later as the symposium seems to have become much less
focussed on generating a group ethic for men of military age.

# Chapter 5

## Collecting and Scholarship

This chapter is designed to explore the way in which Greek vases have been collected, and the ways in which they are studied and published. Our Ajax and Achilles amphora (Fig. 1) is an excellent example of a vase which has, as we have seen, a status as an archaeological object with some significance for the study of the culture which produced and the culture which eventually received it, a part of a museum collection displaying other examples, and as a subtle and moving work of art. It is part of the history of collecting and connoisseurship, of scholarship and research, and also of the reception of the classical world in a later context.

### A potted history of collecting

The Ajax and Achilles vase was found in an Etruscan tomb at Vulci in what is now Tuscany; in this it has much in common with a large proportion of the current holdings of Italian and other European Museums. It could be said that the history of collecting Greek vases as art has its origins in the fact that the Greeks in general, and the Corinthians and Athenians in particular, both colonised and exported much of their pottery abroad, and especially to Etruria, where the Etruscans of the seventh to fourth centuries BC were a keen and receptive market for them and buried them intact in their chamber tombs. They were also strongly enough influenced by what they imported to begin producing their own versions, which soon cease to be copies, both of Corinthian animal styles, and later of Athenian black- and red-figure.

The survival of Roman antiquities in Italy ensured a continuing interest in antiquity itself from mediaeval times, even if understanding of what the antiquities were was very imperfect by modern standards, and by the sixteenth century AD excavation of a sort had begun. In the early stages the interest was mainly in statuary, which found its way into the collections and grand houses of the Italian and eventually other European aristocracy; later, the painted tombs of Etruria and their frequently spectacular contents began to be better known, and to be looted, and Greek pots, then identified as Etruscan, began to appear in some collections, as did the contents of tombs in the Naples area. By the eighteenth century, there was a developed taste in Europe for classical architecture and artefacts. The architecture was copied or inspired designs for grand houses and official buildings. The artefacts began to travel across Europe and eventually to America, not only as antiquities for scholarly investigation, but as desirable components of interior decoration, or collectibles which were also a sign of status. This fuelled a highly competitive market in ancient antiquities, of which finds from Vulci formed a part, in the early nineteenth century. It is likely that our amphora found its way to the Vatican collection, with a number of others from the same area, around 1830, while active acquisition was at its peak.

Eighteenth-century scholars began to recognise Greek vases as Greek rather than Etruscan, but they also began to recognise their diversity of style and origin, and to publish them in formats which are recognisably the ancestors of modern publication habits. It is probable that the taste for collecting and studying Greek vases was fuelled and greatly reinforced by Sir William Hamilton's publication of his two collections, acquired during his appointment as British Envoy to the Kingdom of the Two Sicilies from 1764 to 1800. The publications appeared first in 1776-7, under the supervision of P.V. Hugues D'Hancarville, and secondly in 1791-95, under Wilhelm Tischbein. Both publications show the figured scenes as if they were flat art, partly with the intention of making the plates capable of removal and framing for hanging on the wall, and neither is entirely accurate about what it shows. The earlier publication does, however, show profile drawings of the pots themselves, and is therefore a forerunner of later scholarly publication.

Hamilton collected both by purchase and by excavation; financial constraints impelled the sale of his first collection to the British Parliament, and in 1772 the British Museum became the first public gallery to exhibit Greek vases. From then on, particularly in the nineteenth and early twentieth centuries, the large collections of Europe, and eventually America, private and public, followed suit, and increased accessibility made possible the upsurge of publication and academic study which characterises the way in which Greek vases were treated in this period. Nineteenth- and early twentieth-century scholarship laid the foundations for most of the kinds of publication in which Greek vases appear, and also for the ways in which they are classified, dated and interpreted. In particular, the recognition of local fabrics and their distinctive styles, mainly by eye, but later also by chemical analysis of the clay and the interpretation of their imagery, became extremely sophisticated and not uncontroversial.

The major fabrics began to be distinguished in the early nineteenth century in the wake of increasing discoveries in Italy; Attic and South Italian fabrics, in particular, received detailed attention from the distinguished German scholar Eduard Gerhard, who began to classify vessels by style, and to view style as an indicator of chronological development; his first attempts to do this were published in 1831. His successors were able to distinguish Corinthian, Laconian, and a range of East Greek fabrics, and to work on dates, stylistic similarities and cross-influences between local schools. Recognition of chronologically-related styles, Geometric and Orientalising in particular, became more widespread; by the late nineteenth century scholars such as Furtwängler were deeply concerned with the establishment of a consensus about local origins and the evidence for trade and population movement such knowledge provides; the study of stylistic development further fuelled discussion about chronologies. The recognition of further local fabrics, such as Boiotian in the 1880s, added to the impetus to excavate, especially in Greece itself.

Attic black- and red-figure attracted attention, as we have seen, at least from the mid-eighteenth century, as styles which could be viewed as making a serious contribution to art history. Red-figure, in particular, generated publications which analysed painting styles and commented on subject matter. Attempts to establish schools and painters on the basis of the vases emerged in the last quarter of the nineteenth century; signatures on the pots certainly led to an early set of assumptions about identities and relationships between makers, many of which have of course been challenged since.

Euphronios was one of the earliest painters to receive a monograph, by W. Klein, in 1879; other scholars followed suit, particularly A. Furtwängler, who, with K. Reichhold, published accurate full-size drawings from what they considered to be the most important vases from 1900-32. Furtwängler also distinguished painters by graphic style rather than relying on signatures. Beazley's earliest publications appeared in 1908-11; he was already using an excellent eye and visual memory to make the thousands of attributions on which modern vase-studies are now based; he continued to do so, with increasing acceptance of his methods by the scholarly community, until his death in 1970. More recent scholarship has raised some questions about his aims, methods and influence, but by and large his attribution framework remains the essential tool on which contemporary work on Greek vases, and Athenian vases in particular, is based.

It is sometimes claimed that Beazley's attribution system effectively created a hierarchy of value which was used, to the detriment of archaeological research, by the art and antiquities market, and which seriously distorts both the value of the pots and their proper preservation and study. It is interesting to notice that Sir William Burrell, towards the end of a long collecting career in the late 1940s, clearly decided that Greek vases were a missing but highly desirable class of object in his very distinguished collection, and set out to acquire some. By that stage most of the material of high quality had gone directly or indirectly into the large museums, but, as in fact there still is, there was a good deal on the market of interest and quality, and his collection was enhanced by some representative and attractive examples.

Pots of high quality do still emerge onto the market from time to time, more usually already known and privately collected than not. Formidable international legislation now tends to restrict free art markets in antiquities, so that most newly-discovered items tend to arrive in public collections, not least because current excavation theory keeps Greek with the other finds from the context in which they were found, and so, once recorded, they migrate into museum collections for storage or display as part of the outcome of the excavation.

**How we see Greek vases now**

How do these vases reach public attention now? The pots themselves, overwhelmingly, appear in the museums of the world, though the sort of display they fuel has changed radically in the last half-century. Originally they were displayed as a close descendant of the early-modern grand house collection – the product of a mixture of the collecting instinct, informed or not, and the desire to have them on display, perhaps incorporated into the decor of the house as evidence of cutting-edge style, erudition and culture – a status symbol. In the British Museum, as late as the early 1960s, for example, the principle was to get as many of them on display as possible, and ostensibly for reasons of space they were displayed in cases on shelves in serried ranks, as objects in their own right, without context, or, often, explanatory labels.

It now comes as a surprise to find a principal display (as opposed to one designed for informed reference) which still looks like that, after quite a long period in which a more select body of pots have played a part in a contextual display, with other kinds of object from their chronological period and geographical origin, together with text-boards, maps and comparative photographs of other related material not in the museum's possession. This sort of display was, of course, much more difficult to do, but it also clearly represented a paradigm shift in professional attitudes to

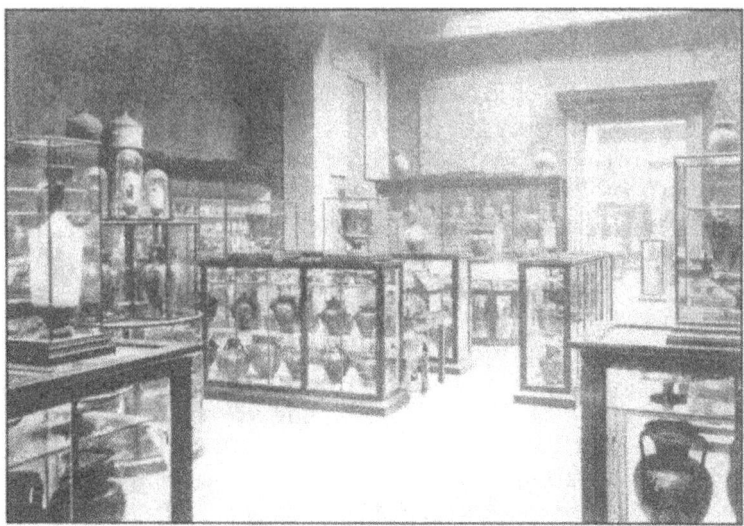

Fig. 47. A vase gallery in the British Museum as it looked in the nineteenth century.

the pots which runs parallel to the way in which they were and are treated for publication purposes. An attitude to display which treated them as objects in their own right, but also as components in a large developmental series, was replaced by one which treated them as a category of evidence for a human culture in all its diversity. That happened in large collections, and in fact in small ones too – three or four of the pots in the collection of the Hunterian Museum in the University of Glasgow appeared in its first integrated display, which aimed to chart the progress of human evolution as a process of socialisation, using items from its zoological, medical, ethnographic, scientific and culture-specific object collections in a more or less chronological sequence.

When the museum collection is big enough, the museum can, of course, run a culture-specific display, like the primary ones currently in the British Museum, and it can also have its cake and eat it by displaying some of its all-time greats, however defined and whether rightly so or not. The mid-1970s saw the re-constitution of many of the earlier forms of pot-specific display in many museum collections into a version of the contextual type; so usual did this become that the occasional reversion to displaying only a version of the serried ranks style, in conventionally packed cases, is hard to view as anything other than a retrograde step.

**Publication habits**

Looking at the pots themselves is the most important way of under-standing them, but interpreting and studying them also leads to writing about them. We saw in Chapter 1 that that they provide archaeological evidence and visual insights for our understanding of Greek culture. We also saw that they have provided inspiration for many other kinds of study and creative practice. There are several important kinds of publication which use and interpret Greek pots for a number of different purposes and audiences. Even these have changed or evolved over time and it is worth thinking about the ways in which they have themselves influenced the ways in which we think about the pots themselves, and how we should treat them.

This is not a comprehensive list, but if I discuss a few kinds of publication, it should outline a view of the situation. Archaeological approaches first:

First, of course, there is the archaeological site-report, which until fairly recently essentially simply reported on the finds of a site, often very extensively and not necessarily without analysis of the finds, but which aimed at publishing the information for the excavators and others to use as bias-free research material. This occasionally attracts adverse criticism on the grounds that it is not to be viewed as true research, and does not attempt to interrogate the larger picture, or induce a radically new mode of thought or method.

There is also the site-report which results from a more contemporary style of excavation or field survey which started because its originator had some research questions to ask, if not answer.

Both of these will think in terms of quantities of material allowing for analysis of various kinds of patterns, most of them with a chronological framework, often allied to a geographical one. The painted Greek vase will form a small and largely un-individualised part of the publication. There are, of course, exceptions – the reports on the excavations of the Athenian agora to name but one, and there the pot-volumes have created typologies, and in one case at least, an approach to interpreting a very specific set of assemblages of pots for the post-Classical symposium in a social and historical context.

Then there are explicitly art-historical approaches to the study of vases, and these are often the way in which students of Classical Civilisation become familiar with Greek vases and their cultural context.

An important type of publication for students, and perhaps the essential guide to finding our way at the start, is the handbook, which either deals with the history of single or multiple ceramic fabrics chronologically, or incorporates it into histories of Greek art; good examples, such as the Thames and Hudson *World of Art* series, have many illustrations and an informative commentary, which deals systematically with technical aspects, decorative content, painters, shapes, and the historical and social context in which the pots were used. Histories of ancient or Greek art use fewer examples, and situate them alongside other works in other media and materials, so that they can be compared with contemporary sculpture, and other types of decorative art. In this kind of context, some painted vases are used as a basis of speculation about the nature of painting in other media, such as wall paintings, of which there are very few surviving examples. The comparative treatment of several kinds of visual art-form often found in this type of book allows for us to develop a sense of period style and technique, and to see how some kinds of technical skill, such as the capacity for suggesting solid objects in a flat medium, developed.

These books treat vases seriously as works of art, in an art-historical context, as do the occasional large-format publications such as Arias, Hirmer and Shefton's *History of Greek Vase Painting*. These foreground glamorous photographs of outstanding individual examples, arranged chronologically and with a good deal of attention to some of the more important painters in Beazley and Trendall's lists; their commentaries reflect both a developmental framework, and excitement about the individual work of art.

We should be aware, though, that not all surveys start from an art-historical perspective. There is also the survey which attempts to avoid art-historical assumptions and tries instead to approach the fabric as if it were any other archaeological artefact, often with considerable success. It may well discuss localised industrial production, usage, and fabrication methods.

Beazley's (and A.D. Trendall's) catalogue volumes are the major and fundamental lists of attributions by painter, workshop and group within the Athenian and South Italian fabrics. These are the essential framework on which contemporary scholarly study of the vases in their ancient context is based, but also, perhaps inevitably, the ancestors and foundations of an approach which treats the vases as a developmental series, and is often found, naturally enough, in the handbook.

Then there are the *Corpus Vasorum Antiquorum* (*CVA* hereafter), and single-painter monographs based around the Beazley and Trendall lists, but with amplification, including the series now known as *Kerameus*. Both of these are essentially object-based: the *CVA* is an internationally sponsored catalogue raisonné of all or part of a museum's holdings, and allows for publication of the pots as individual items, whether or not (often not) they have a recorded archaeological context. Its format has changed slightly over the years; an individual fascicle used to be a portfolio of loose-leaf plates with a commentary. Many of its contributors now recognise that the average user does not possess a library-sized table, or the run of fascicles from which to distribute loose leaves for comparative study on that table, and the average library does not have the staff to clear up and re-constitute the portfolio fascicles afterwards. It is now often a bound volume, which is cheaper to produce anyway, and is gradually evolving towards a web-based format, updatable from the institution which owns the pots. This is perfect for the vast majority of Greek vases, for historical reasons intimately connected with the history of collecting which has had the effect of distancing many Greek vases from their findspots and archaeological context. The series also has connections with another publication-trend, broadly described as reception studies, which are often also an exercise in apologetics for the whole history of museum collecting and acquisition, and its dovetail with the art and antiquities market, both the apparently legal if not ethical, and the overtly illegal.

The *Kerameus* series is dedicated to the single-painter monograph, which treats the oeuvre, or part of the oeuvre, of a given painter in the Beazley/Trendall scheme, as the subject matter of an essay which extends Beazley's already extant principles based on that chronological learning curve to reconstruct the career output of a painter, usually a related workshop, sometimes a group of workshops, or other individuals who might constitute a stylistic context complete with cross-influences, networking, house styles, professional rivalries, pioneers, retardataires, and apprenticeship schemes. Its supporters would defend it by saying that it is a way of getting at what evidence we do have for a small-scale but significant industry and its working structures, and hence at an important area of social history.

This has, at least indirectly, led to two other significant publication trends: the earlier one is that which attacks the study of Greek pots as significant objects of any sort; it began as an extension of a theory of fabricated objects in which the significant factor was the way in which objects shaped and constructed in a particular way, as a natural consequence of the properties of their material, turn up, frequently with less sense of inevitability, in another. For example, the volute krater, which works admirably in metal, is much more fragile as a ceramic vessel, especially its handles, which are easily broken off. Pottery versions – cups are a good example – often imitate in paint the way in which the handles of a metal vessel are attached with rivets through a decorative fitting to the body.

Reflection on this led to a theory of Greek, and especially Athenian, pottery production as an industry in which there were no original crafts-people or artists, because they were all hacks literally copying now virtually non-existent prototypes in much rarer and more precious materials, whose generators were the source of the occasional signatures we find on the surviving ceramics. It is interesting to notice, in passing, that all this ran roughly in parallel with the wider dissemination of literary theories about the death of the author. This approach is now in itself slightly passé, and its more vociferous progenitors (even those interested in reception studies) have moved on to other areas of what is now described as a programme of research into the hierarchy of materials in the ancient world.

The other, and I suspect equally influential, trend in publication is one which has certainly been fun to read, and that is a growing tendency to reflect on what the major movers and shakers of the past did to a subject which has been dominated, until comparatively recently, by a small number of individuals who had ample opportunity to become sacred monsters in the process of inventing, defining, and protecting their corner. The objectives of these studies are nearer to those of the contemporary critical biographer – as one notable practitioner says, 'to question the procedure by which the biographical person is "invented" ' and also the literalism which the standard chronologically-controlled mode induces in the reader's reception of its subject. And it means that we are beginning to be shown the social and political framework of a specialised academic world, and its opportunities for self-construction and disaster via its subject interests, particularly the ones which might, especially in the hands of the professional rubbisher, ensure that for a time at least, attention is focussed away from the objects of study themselves; the interest is in people, not pots. This is understandable in a context in which, largely for financial reasons, we have been trying to stretch people to manage material objects without the need for intimate and trained knowledge of them (and that goes for making as well as understanding them) and thereby to stop training, employing and paying experts.

Fortunately, many of the standard publication formats do have an ongoing use for the professional, and recent personal experience suggests that Greek vases and their pictures continue to provoke an intense response in students and viewing public alike. They are objects which can speak with an eloquent voice, if allowed to do so.

# Where to see Greek Vases

In Britain the largest collection, with the widest range of types of vase, is in the British Museum, which currently shows its holdings both in contextual displays by period, and as comparative displays of the pots themselves. Its range is very wide, and there is plenty to satisfy curiosity from any of the angles of approach implied by this book. A further advantage of this collection is that the museum also has large holdings of other kinds of Greek art and artefact, displayed both typologically and contextually.

There are also substantial collections in the Ashmolean Museum in Oxford, the Fitzwilliam Museum in Cambridge, and the National Museum of Scotland in Edinburgh. There are smaller collections, often of some distinction, in many municipal and university museums – the Marischal Museum of the University of Aberdeen, the Burrell Collection and the Hunterian Museum in Glasgow, the Shefton Museum of the University of Newcastle upon Tyne, the Royal Pump Room Museum in Harrogate, and the Ure Museum of the University of Reading among them.

Outside Britain, the major European collections are in the Louvre in Paris; the Rijksmuseum in Leiden; the Antikensammlung in Munich, the Charlottenburg in Berlin, the Martin von Wagner Museum in Würzburg; in Italy the Vatican Museums and the Villa Giulia in Rome, and the Museo Nazionale in Naples; in Greece itself, the National Museum in Athens. In America, the major collection is in the Metropolitan Museum in New York, and there are impressive holdings in the Museum of Fine Art in Boston.

Most of these museums have websites which illustrate the highlights of their collections. The website Perseus http://www.perseus.tufts.edu/ and the online Beazley Archive http://www.beazley.ox.ac.uk are both major digital resources with thousands of images. The latter is a specialised searchable database.

# Suggestions for Further Reading

Greek vases, unlike sculpture, were not treated in antiquity as art which generated critical commentary, or biographies of the makers, so there are no ancient sources, and the bibliography below consists of modern literature about them. In fact there is a great deal of material in print, so this is a very selective list.

**1. Handbooks.** The following handbooks are extremely fully illustrated, with a helpful commentary and suggestions for further and more specialised reading, and are available in paperback. They are excellent reference and information tools:

J. Boardman, *Early Greek Vase Painting* (London 1998)
J. Boardman, *Athenian Black Figure Vases* (London 1974)
J. Boardman, *Athenian Red Figure Vases: the Archaic Period* (London 1976)
J. Boardman, *Athenian Red Figure Vases: the Classical Period* (London 1989)
J. Boardman, *The History of Greek Vases* (London 2001)
A.D. Trendall, *Red Figure Vases of Southern Italy and Sicily* (London 1989)

**2. Discussion.** The following provide discussion and critique of the approaches assumed by the handbooks above:

T. Rasmussen, N. Spivey, *Looking at Greek Vases* (Cambridge 1991)
B.A. Sparkes, *Greek Pottery: An Introduction* (Manchester 1991)
B.A. Sparkes, *The Red and the Black* (London 1996)
R.M. Cook, *Greek Painted Pottery*, 3rd edn (London 1997)

**3. Pictures.** The first two titles below provide both large-scale photographs and a scholarly commentary. The *Corpus Vasorum Antiquorum* provides very full factual coverage and photographs of vases in the contributing collections, but is less accessible to students at school or undergraduate level.

P. Arias, M. Hirmer, B.B. Shefton, *A History of Greek Vase Painting* (London 1963)

M. Hirmer, E. Simon, *Die Griechischen Vasen* (Munich 1976)

*Corpus Vasorum Antiquorum*, fascicles from 1926, by country and museum

The books listed below are more advanced, and although they underlie much of what has been said in the text of this book, they are not primary texts for students at the early stages of study.

**4. Typologies.** These are some of the important, but more advanced typological catalogues, which underlie the handbooks:

D.A. Amyx, *Corinthian Vase-Painting of the Archaic Period* (California 1998)

J.D. Beazley, *Attic Black Figure Vases* (Oxford 1956)

J.D. Beazley, *Attic Red Figure Vases* (Oxford 1963)

J.D. Beazley, *Paralipomena* (Oxford 1971)

H.A. Brijder, *Siana Cups I and Komast Cups* (Amsterdam 1983)

J.N. Coldstream, *Greek Geometric Pottery* (London 1968)

A.D. Trendall, *The Red-figured Vases of Lucania, Campania and Sicily* (Oxford 1967)

A.D. Trendall & A. Cambitoglou, *The Red-figured Vases of Apulia* (Oxford 1978ff.)

A.D. Trendall, *The Red-figured Vases of Paestum* (Rome 1987)

**5. Art-historical discussion of fabrics or painters.** These are examples of much more focussed and in-depth discussions of the styles and painters concerned.

J.D. Beazley, *The Development of Attic Black Figure* (California 1951, 1986)

L. Burn, *The Meidias Painter* (Oxford 1987)

E. Böhr, *Der Schaukelmaler* (Mainz 1982)

J. Hemelrijk, *Caeretan Hydriai* (Mainz 1984)

K. Kilinski, *Boiotian Black Figure Vase Painting of the Archaic Period* (Mainz 1990)

D.C. Kurtz, *Athenian White Lekythoi* (Oxford 1975)

S. Morris, *The Black and White Style* (Yale 1984)

H. Payne, *Protokorinthische Vasenmalerei* (Berlin 1933)

H. Payne, *Necrocorinthia* (Oxford 1931)

Martin Robertson, *The Art of Vase Painting in Classical Athens* (Cambridge 1992)

**6. Iconography.** These concentrate on the exploration of mythical and other subject matter. The volume by Carpenter is in the same series as the handbooks in the first list, and is very fully illustrated

C. Bérard, *A City of Images* (Princeton 1989)
T.H. Carpenter, *Art and Myth in Ancient Greece* (London 1991)
K. Schefold, *Myth and Legend in Early Greek Art* (London 1966)
S. Woodford, *Images of Myths in Classical Antiquity* (Cambridge 2003)

**6. Technique**

J.V. Noble, *The Techniques of Attic Painted Pottery* (New York, London, 1966, 1985)

**7. Trade**

A.W. Johnston, *Trademarks on Greek Vases* (London 1979)

**8. Chronology**

W.R. Biers, *Art, Artefacts and Chronology in Classical Archaeology* (London 1992)

**9. Critique.** These two volumes approach the study of Greek vases from a critical angle, and ask why we look at them in the way we do. They suggest other approaches.

A. Snodgrass, *An Archaeology of Greece* (California 1987)
M. Vickers, D. Gill, *Artful Crafts: ancient Greek silverware and pottery* (Oxford 1994)

**10. Biography.** These are examples of the biographical study of scholars who have influenced the study of Greek vases, discussed briefly in Chapter 5.

M. Beard, *The Invention of Jane Harrison* (Cambridge, Mass. 2000)
P. Rouet, *Approaches to the Study of Attic Vases: Beazley and Pottier* (Oxford 2001)

# Suggestions for Further Study

A visit to the Greek galleries in the British Museum or any of the larger museums noted above will reveal how much material there is, and how selective and limited this book has had to be. The large museums usually have more than one work by Beazley's named painters, so one focus of interest could be to study the stylistic links between the paintings from the pots themselves, which is always more rewarding than using photographs. Seeing for yourself gives a much better idea of scale and colour, and a sense of the decorated vessel as a whole.

A second useful and enjoyable study in a museum which has sculpture holdings too, as the British Museum does, is to try to compare the drawing styles of the vases with the sculptures of a comparable date. The painters who were working in the latter half of the fifth century BC in Athens were clearly aware of the Parthenon, and some of their figures are very closely related to what they could see in its sculptural scheme.

Here are a few suggestions, related to the chapters of this book:

*1. Greek Vases and Time*: try sketching the profiles of differently dated examples of a particular shape of vase in a museum with enough to allow at least five different ones. Cups and amphorae are particularly rewarding, especially their rims and feet. Is it possible to see any general evolutionary tendencies in the way shapes change? Are there any local shapes which transfer to other centres of production? Are there any which remain localised?

*2. Painters and Potters*: study the entry on the Pioneer Group (Euphronios, Euthymides and their workshop) in John Boardman, *Athenian Red-figure Vases, the Archaic Period*, 29ff. with the pictures. Do you think that Beazley was right to see them as a workshop of painters who all knew each other? What are the links he could identify? Are you convinced?

*3. Shapes and their Uses*: think about the symposium, and the kinds of picture which appear on its pottery. How do you think that the myths which were used were meant to contribute to the mood of the party? Were there different kinds of occasion to which some scenes were better suited than others?

*4. Scenes and Storytelling*: think about the scenes of real life which appear on Greek vases. What is real about the life depicted on them? Are they to be treated as documentary or ideal? Think about the kinds of myth which are shown: why these myths? Why are some more popular, or at least frequent, than others?

*5. Collecting and Scholarship*: do you have a sense of the fascination Greek vases have exercised on their fans? What was it which led those who were able to do so to assemble collections of them from the sixteenth century AD onwards? Why did Beazley create his attribution system at the point at which he did? How far have the available types of publication conditioned the way in which we think about Greek vases? What further ways of studying them might there be in the future?

# Glossary

**aegis**: a poncho fringed with snakes, which bestows invisibility on the wearer; often worn by Athene.

**alabastron**: a scent-bottle, usually used by women, shaped like an elongated tear-drop or pear, originating in Egypt, where it was often made of alabaster (see Fig. 23).

**amphora**: two-handled jar (see Fig. 23). See also *Panathenaic amphora* below.

**aryballos**: a scented oil bottle, usually used by men, normally spherical, occasionally pointed in shape (see Fig. 23).

**Attic**: from Athens or its surrounding territory, or a style originating there.

**bilingual**: indicating a vase painted in both black-figure and red-figure.

**chiton**: a version of the tunic worn by both sexes, short for men, long for women; the female version is normally fastened along the shoulder and arm with a series of buttons or pins.

**Corinthian**: from Corinth or its surrounding territory, or a style originating there.

**dinos**: a *krater* with a round bottom, usually with a stand.

**Geometric**: an early Iron Age style of pottery which uses geometric patterns and related stylised figures; occasionally the term is extended to mean the period in which it was made.

**herm**: a carved pillar supporting either a bust of a god, originally Hermes, or later, a portrait; if the head represented Hermes, the pillar often displayed a set of genitalia halfway down. Many Athenian houses had one beside the main door; others were displayed in the agora or main square of the city.

**himation**: a cloak worn by both sexes, but often by men without a *chiton* underneath.

**hydria**: a three-handled water jar (see Fig. 23).

**kalpis**: a version of the *hydria* with curved sides (see Fig. 23).

**kantharos**: a tall cup with high-swung handles, often carried by Dionysos or Herakles.

**kithara**: a stringed instrument used for formal performance.

**kline**: a piece of furniture which could be used as a sofa, a bed, or a bier.

**kottabos**: a party game involving flicking the remains of the wine in the bottom of the cup at a target.

**kotyle**: a form of drinking cup, roughly equivalent to a beer mug (see Fig. 23).

**krater**: the central mixing bowl used at the symposium – the bell krater, column krater, volute krater and calyx krater are variants on the basic shape, distinguished by the shape of the body or the handles (see Fig. 23).

**kyathos**: a ceremonial ladle (see Fig. 24).

**kylix**: a two-handled shallow cup (see Fig. 23).

**lebes**: a general word for a large bowl or basin, occasionally an alternative word for a *dinos* (see Fig. 23).

**lekythos**: an oil bottle, larger than the *aryballos* or the *alabastron*, often used in burial ceremonies (see Fig. 23).

**lotus**: a stylised flower, usually shown as a bud; often forms a repeated element of a chain with *palmettes* (see Fig. 1).

**loutrophoros**: a specialised tall water jar, with two or three handles, used for rituals such as weddings or funerals (see Fig. 23).

**maeander**: otherwise known as Greek key pattern.

**metope**: the square panel, usually with sculptured figures repeated between the blocks with three grooves known as triglyphs, which is a component on the frieze of a Doric temple; by extension, a square picture-space.

**oinochoe**: a wine jug (see Fig. 23).

**Orientalising**: the pottery style, partly derived from Near Eastern decorative ideas, which follows *Geometric*, and by extension, the period in which it was made.

**palmette**: a stylised palm-leaf which often forms a chain pattern alternating with a lotus (see Fig. 1).

**Panathenaic amphora**: an *amphora* of a specialised pointed shape, with decoration relating it to its function as the container for the oil given as a prize in the Panathenaic games in Athens (see Fig. 23).

**pelike**: a form of amphora with a sagging belly (see Fig. 23).

**peplos**: the alternative to a *chiton*, normally a long tunic worn by women, with a single fastening on each shoulder.

**Protocorinthian**: the earliest Orientalising style of Corinthian pottery decoration.

**Protogeometric**: a pre-Geometric style of pottery decoration, usually using bands and concentric circles.

**psykter**: a mushroom-shaped cooler vase which should sit inside a *krater* (see Fig. 23, not to scale).

**pyxis**: a pottery box, often cylindrical (see Fig. 23).

**skyphos**: an alternative word for a *kotyle*.

**tondo**: a circular picture in the bottom of the inside of a cup.

# Index

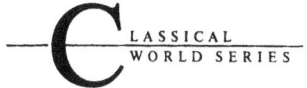

# CLASSICAL WORLD SERIES

RECENT TITLES IN THE CLASSICAL WORLD SERIES
(for a full list see opposite title page)

# Athletics in the Ancient World

Zahra Newby

ISBN 1 85399 688 2

The athletic competitions that took place during festivals such as that at Olympia, or within the confines of city gymnasia, were a key feature of life in ancient Greece. From the commemoration of victorious athletes in poetry or sculpture to the archaeological remains of baths, gymnasia and stadia, surviving evidence offers plentiful testimony to the importance of athletic activity in Greek culture, and its survival well into Roman times.

This book offers an introduction to the many forms that athletics took in the ancient world, and to the sources of evidence by which we can study it. As well as looking at the role of athletics in archaic and classical Greece, it also covers the less-explored periods of the Hellenistic and Roman worlds. Many different aspects of athletics are considered – not only the well-known contests of athletic festivals, but also the place of athletic training within civic education and military training, and its integration into the bathing culture of the Roman world.

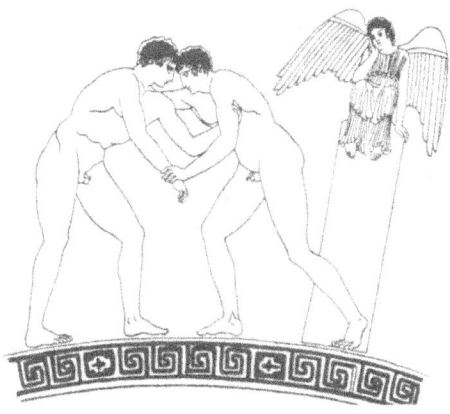

# The Plays of Sophocles

A.F. Garvie

ISBN 1 85399 680 7

The emphasis throughout this concise, informative and stimulating book is on Sophocles' tragic thinking, on the concept of the 'Sophoclean hero', and on the dramatic structure of the plays. Seven studies of the individual plays make up the book, drawn together by a brief concluding chapter.

*The Plays of Sophocles* aims to help readers to understand why Sophocles is still worth reading, or going to see in the theatre, in the twenty-first century, and to show how far Sophoclean scholarship has moved in recent decades from the once prevalent view that he was a pious religious conformist who had nothing very profound or original to say, but who said it very beautifully.

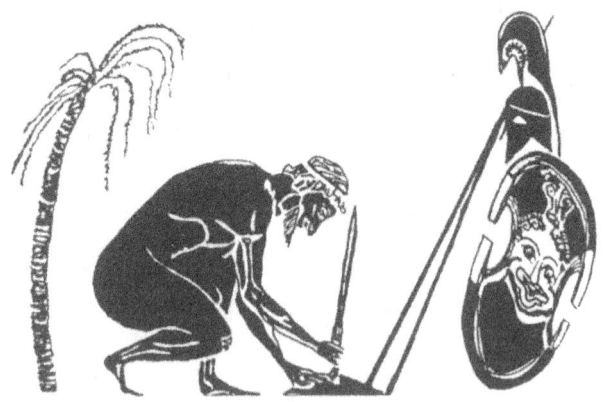

# The Plays of Euripides

James Morwood

ISBN 1 85399 614 9

No book on all the plays of Euripides has been published since 1967. In the meantime there has been a revolution in the way we view not only classical drama generally, but this particular dramatist.

As well as reflecting this revolution, *The Plays of Euripides* seeks to show that the playwright was constantly reinventing himself. A truly Protean figure, he set out on a new journey in each of the nineteen plays. Short essays on all of them are rounded off by an epilogue which identifies some underlying themes but continues to insist on the diversity of this great dramatist.

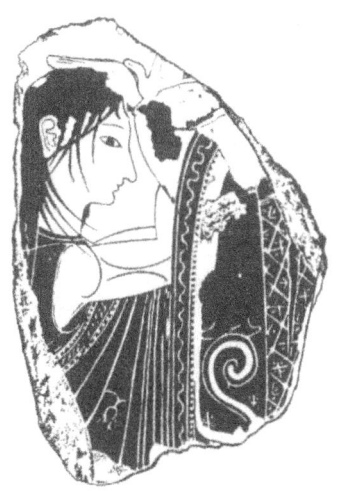

# The Greek and Roman Historians

Timothy E. Duff

ISBN 1 85399 601 7

What did 'history' mean to the Greeks and Romans? What were the aims of the ancient historians and how did they evaluate their sources? This volume traces the development of conceptions of history and its practice from Homer to the writers of the Roman Empire. It serves as an introduction to the great historians of the ancient world and contains sections on Herodotos, Thucydides, Xenophon, Polybios, Sallust, Livy, Velleius, Tacitus, Suetonius, Plutarch, Arrian and Dio, as well as on some other historians whose work now survives only in fragments.

Brief analyses of the events which form the background to each historian's work set the writers in their historical context. Each section is self-contained and may be read on its own; but specific attention is paid to links between the different historians, and the ways in which they were influenced by or competed with one another.

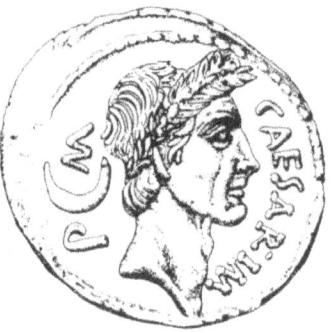

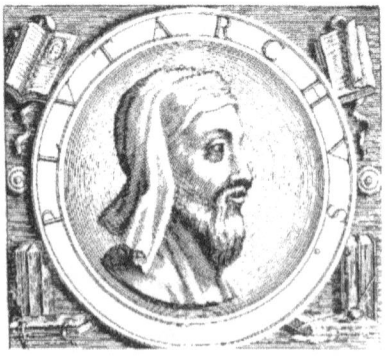

# Art and the Romans

Anne Haward

1 85399 558 4

Is there more to Roman art than mosaics? What did the Romans look for in their portraits? Was there impressionist painting before the Impressionists? This survey for the general student looks at the art created for and by the Romans and what they wanted from it.

In place of the usual historical outline approach, *Art and the Romans* looks at the subject by genre; the Romans' appreciation of painting, sculpture and the decorative arts, in a society where the majority of work was commissioned, was different from that of the present day. Art in a world without printing or photography to spread visual images meant much more direct contact with the artist and influence by the patron. Drawing on literary sources as well as illustrations from many parts of the Roman world, this survey up to the time of Constantine considers what Romans hoped to achieve and how far they were successful. Included are suggestions for further study, a bibliography and recommended sites to view the art discussed.

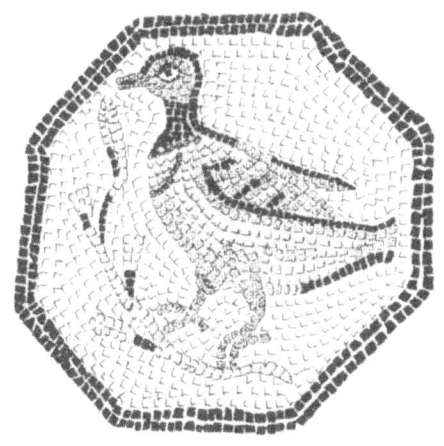

*Books of related interest:*

# An Introduction to Greek Art

### Susan Woodford

0 7156 2095 9

*251 illustrations*

The fragments of Greek sculpture and vase painting that have survived into the twentieth century are like pieces of a shattered mirror reflecting the former glory of Greek art. Though some of the images are obviously beautiful, others require interpretation before their true quality can become apparent. This book, designed primarily as an introduction for students, helps the reader trace the development of Greek art in the immensely creative period from the eighth to the fourth century BC – the period between the composition of the Homeric poems and the conquest of Alexander the Great. Important works are generously illustrated and lucidly analysed, so that an integrated picture of Greek art emerges.

# The Trojan War in Ancient Art

### Susan Woodford

0 7156 2468 7

*113 illustrations*

The myths of the Trojan war captured the imagination not only of Greek and Roman authors – Homer, Euripides, Virgil, Ovid and many others – but also of countless Greek and Roman painters and sculptors. This handsomely illustrated book brings to life the literary and, above all, the visual traditions.

Susan Woodford is an engaging guide, as concerned with nuances of human experience as with aesthetic detail. By perceptively analysing a variety of representations, she assesses the creative solutions individual artists found to problems posed by the narrative; by comparing verbal and pictorial treatments of telling episodes, she demonstrates the liberating flexibility of Greek mythology.

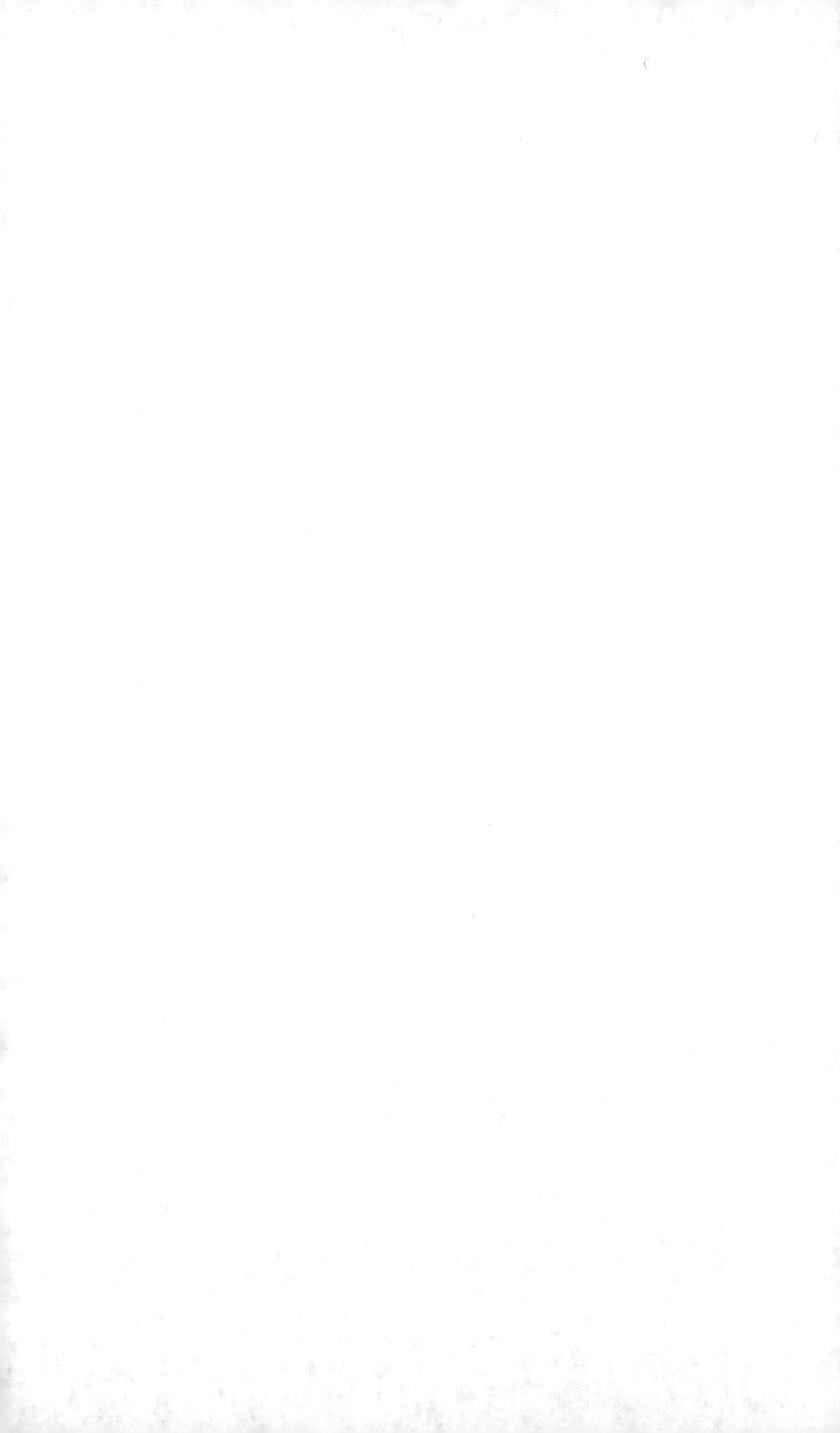